The Observer's Pocket Series
MOTORCYCLES

The Observer's Book of
MOTORCYCLES

ROBERT M. CROUCHER

FREDERICK WARNE & CO LTD

FREDERICK WARNE & CO INC

LONDON : NEW YORK

© Frederick Warne & Co Ltd
London, England
1976

Library of Congress Catalog Card No. 76-2245

ISBN 0 7232 1554 5

*Printed in Great Britain by
Butler & Tanner Ltd
Frome*
606.1175

Introduction

It is appropriate that the first edition of *The Observer's Book of Motorcycles* should appear during a period when these machines are enjoying a popular revival. The motorcycle appeared on the scene at the same time as the motor car yet it has frequently lost ground in the face of the relentless growth of private car ownership – although there are still many countries where the number of motorcycles outstrips the volume of cars.

For a long time motorcycles were designed as a tough and exacting form of transport only for enthusiasts, but since the 1960s they have changed their image. Today, as the pages of this book show, they can be highly sophisticated examples of motor-vehicle technology, utilizing many of the convenience features normally associated with the motor car. Nevertheless the increasing popularity of dual-purpose and off-road machines shows that there is still a strong demand for the rugged no-frills motorcycling that offers simple and cheap transportation in town or country.

Apart from the big touring superbikes and off-road machines, much of the increase in two-wheelers can be explained by the demand for mopeds and lightweight commuter models. The use of 'step-thru' frames and small, reliable and economic engines has resulted in an ideal vehicle for the commuter wishing to beat the traffic jams or to save on the cost of personal transport; and the moped offers the youngster a first taste of fun and freedom while gaining the traffic experience required later for the bigger bikes or motor cars.

Purists may be wondering why mopeds or any machine under 125 cc are included in a book on motorcycles, but the distinction is becoming increasingly difficult to sustain. Many of the modern mopeds not only look like motorcycles but perform like motorcycles, and because they are often a stepping stone to the big bikes they will be of interest to the reader. One problem which does arise from including mopeds and scooters is that there are so many under 50 cc models available. For space reasons some selection has become inevitable, but even so, this first edition manages to feature more than 50 manufacturers and over 200 models.

The public tends to possess extreme views about motorcycles; there are the two-wheel enthusiasts and those that see these machines as dirty, dangerous nuisances on our roads. Mindful of the need to preserve a good public image, I hope the reader will not object to being advised that in the hands of the inexperienced a motorcycle can be a danger to road users and an indiscreet intrusion on the general environment. Indeed, faced with the facts of the high accident rate among young motorcyclists, the industry has helped set up the Schools' Traffic Education Programme (STEP) which, in liaison with the Road Safety Departments of local authorities, has designed proper training for young people in the use of mopeds and motorcycles. This book will contribute if it gives the reader a greater awareness of the many motorcycles available and their possibilities.

I should like to thank the many manufacturers and their UK concessionaires for the information and assistance that they have so freely given to make this book possible.

Robert M. Croucher

Key to Technical Specifications

ENGINE
Type   Motorcycle engines come in single- or multi-cylinder form and as 4-strokes, 2-strokes, rotaries and even electrically driven. In the 4-stroke engine power results from four movements of the piston (Induction — petrol/air mixture drawn into the cylinder; Compression — mixture compressed; Power — mixture ignited; Exhaust — exhaust gas ejected) while in the 2-stroke combustion takes place on every ascent of the piston. In rotary engines triangular rotors sweep a specially shaped chamber (epitrochoidal) to provide variable compression and combustion spaces.
Bore × Stroke   The relationship between cylinder diameter and the length of movement of the piston within it. Where the dimensions are roughly the same the engine is said to be 'square'.
Capacity   The piston displacement of the engine in cubic centimetres. It can be calculated from the formula — bore radius^2 × 3.142 × stroke × the number of cylinders. (10 mm = 1 cm.)
Compression ratio   Indicates the extent to which combustion gases are squeezed as the piston reaches its top-most position (TDC) by comparing the volume of space left above the piston and the cylinder swept volume. The trend towards shorter stroke engines for motorcycles has led to an increase in compression ratios.
Carburettors   The number of carburettors, the choke size diameter and the make are given.
Maximum power   This is the brake horsepower (**bhp**) of the engine and the engine speed (rpm) at which this is achieved. This figure varies with the methods used to measure it. The German DIN standard measures the net output of the engine under normal use, while SAE figures may be test-bed results ignoring the operation of accessories like pumps and generators. The figures quoted are manufacturers' claimed figures and SAE measures are starred*
Fuel tank   Figures in litres normally include the reserve where provided.

TRANSMISSION
Gears/Clutch   The number of gears and the type of clutch is given. **wmp**=wet multi-plate clutch in which small metal and friction discs bathed in oil engage and disengage the drive from the engine to the rear wheel. **dsp**=dry single plate clutch, a type commonly fitted to cars and normally only found on bigger bikes. **A**=automatic clutch and is mostly found on low-powered mopeds. The speeding up of the engine automatically engages the clutch as centrifugal force builds up on the pressure plate, and drive is only completely disconnected when the engine speed falls to idling.

Electrical
Ignition   Voltage system (6 or 12)/Ampere-hour capacity of the battery where fitted/the type of ignition system (magneto, b&c=battery and coil, ε=electronic)/charging system (A=alternator, A.C.; D=dynamo, D.C.).
Starting   Normally by kick-operated crank although mopeds are often started by pedal. Where electric starters are fitted usually a kick start is also provided.

BRAKING
Front/Rear The diameter of the drum (dm) or disc (dc) is given. Drum brakes work by mechanically expanding shoes lined with a friction material against the inner surface of a drum rotating with the wheel. Disc braking is normally achieved by hydraulic means which presses a friction pad against a metal disc bolted to the wheel and revolving with it.
Front tyres Sizes shown are for standard fittings but normally there are many tyre-size options available. The first figure refers to the tyre wicth in inches and the second figure gives the wheel rim diameter in inches. Interestingly tyre measurements are still commonly given in Imperial units. Tyres may be road or trials type, the latter having large, staggered cleats for better traction in loose sand and gravel. Front tyres are normally ribbed to give positive steering and good road holding.
Rear tyres These covers have a curved profile and a deep zig-zag pattern so that they will grip the road when the bike is banked on bends.

SUSPENSION
Front/Rear **T**=telescopic type where the front fork has twin telescoping tubes attached to the front-wheel axle and dampened by coil springs and hydraulic shock absorbers. Sometimes the sliding tubes are covered by protective gaiters. **LL**=leading link forks in which the front wheel is suspended from two pivoting links attached to pressed steel forks and cushioned by spring-type shock absorbers. **SA**=swinging arm rear suspension. The swinging arm fork supports the rear wheel and is hinged to the frame behinc the engine so that when ridden over bumps the rear wheel lifts with the swinging arm and is cushioned by hydraulic shock absorbers. **(3-pos)** indicates that the bike is fitted with a camring adjuster to change the spring pre-load on the rear suspension units to take into account the extra weight of a pillion rider. Normally a maximum of 5 different positions are provided.

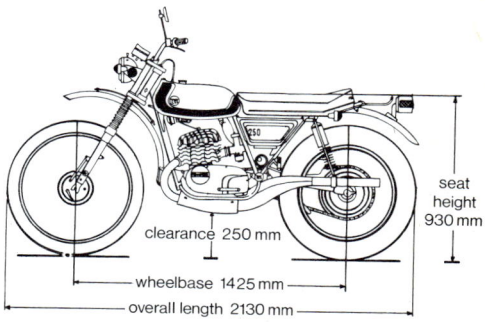

DIMENSIONS
Dry weight As opposed to kerb weight which is the weight of a motorcycle fuelled and oiled for the road. Dry weight provides a basic comparison figure which ignores varying fuel and oil capacities.

PERFORMANCE
Top speed Manufacturers are reluctant to give performance figures for motorcycles because what is achieved can vary between individual machines and much depends on the conditions under which the testing is carried out. Figures given are normally manufacturers' claimed results except where indicated **(p)** which refers to test results from motorcycle press sources. In all cases these figures should only be treated as a general guide.

Fuel consumption Some claims can be very misleading when they are obtained under conditions of steady, low-speed running. These figures based on litres consumption per 100 kilometres are only an approximate guide to what might be obtained under average riding conditions.

NOTES
The photographs show the model to which the technical specification given applies and alternative versions are listed under the heading 'Notes'. Construction and use regulations vary enormously from country to country and there may be considerable variations in the specifications of export models. Normally the specifications used in this book are those applying to the UK market and where a model is not imported into this country its local name is always used.

... Indicates information not available.

Abbreviations and Technical Glossary

Ah Ampere-hours, a measure of the electricity delivered by the battery, e.g. 14 Ah=1 amp for 14 hours or 2 amps for 7 hours.

Amal British make of carburettor also made under licence in Spain.

bhp Brake horse power is the useful power actually available and is measured by causing the engine to work against a dynamometer.

Bing German make of carburettor.

Cafe racer Solo road bike customized in imitation of road-racing machines with fairings, clip-ons and mildly tuned engine.

CDI Capacitor Discharge Ignition uses solid state switching to time the spark at the plug instead of mechanical contact points which need frequent adjustment. Many moto-cross bikes now have it fitted.

Clip-ons Short, racing-style handlebars which are adjustable for rake and height. Clip-on handlebars lower the body profile of the rider, creating the most efficient high speed riding position.

Dell'Orto Famous Italian carburettor manufacturer founded in 1934.

Desmo Short for desmodromic, a method of positively closing engine valves by cams and springs to prevent valve bounce at high speed. It was developed by Fabio Taglioni of Ducati S.p.A. for production bikes, although positive valve control had been patented as early as 1910 by F. H. Arnott.

DIN Deutsche Industrie-Norm.

dohc Double overhead cam. An engine having a separate camshaft for the inlet and exhaust valves mounted in the cylinder head. (See sohc.)

Earles A design of front suspension with long leading links.

Enduro American term for motorcycles equipped to be legally ridden on roads and suitable for cross-country work. These machines have full road lighting with trials-type tyres and high ground clearances. They are also known as Trail bikes – not to be confused with Trial or Moto Cross (MX) machines which are not normally street legal. Some manufacturers seem to use these terms rather loosely in describing their models.

Four Engine with four cylinders.
Gurtner French carburettor make.
Horizontal An engine placed in the frame in a horizontal position. Where two cylinders are opposite each other with the crankshaft between them the engine is said to be horizontally opposed.
IRZ Spanish carburettor manufacturer.
ISDT International Six Days Trial, an international endurance competition held since 1913 for the World Trophy and the Silver Vase award.
Isolastic Trade name for Norton's system of isolating the vibrations from the engine, transmission and rear wheel by using rubber mountings in the frame. (See page 12.)
Jikov Carburettor from Czechoslovakia.
Keihin Japanese carburettor manufacturer.
Magneto Self-contained ignition-spark generating instrument. On 2-strokes it is often fixed to the flywheel.
Mikuni Japanese make of carburettor.
Minarelli Italian 2-stroke engine manufacturer.
Italian 2-stroke engine manufacturer.
Moped A machine of under 50 cc equipped with pedals by means of which it may be propelled. Regulations one use vary from country to country, and in Italy and France, for example, such machines can be ridden by fourteen-year-olds without any form of licence or test.
Reed-valve A 2-stroke cylinder valve arrangement developed by Suzuki, in which induction pressure causes a flapper-type valve to open and close the intake port. The low-speed torque and fuel economy of a reed-valve engine are claimed to be better than an equivalent piston-port engine.
Rotary-valve A refinement of the basic piston-port 2-stroke engine in which the opening and closing of the intake port is controlled by the rotation of a thin, circular disc keyed to the crankshaft and piston position. This system permits fine control of intake port timing and can give increased power and good fuel economy.
Sachs Famous German 2-stroke engine manufacturer, Fichtel & Sachs AG, Schweinfurt, now part of the Guest, Keen and Nettlefold group.
SAE Society of Automotive Engineers.
Shaft drive Final drive by rotating shaft rather than roller chain.
Single Engine with one cylinder.
Sohc Single overhead cam engine where one camshaft carries both the inlet and exhaust cams. Known as a 'single knocker'.
Step-thru Underbone frame design used for mopeds and lightweights, making it unnecessary to lift the leg over the saddle when mounting.
TDC Top dead centre is the top-most position of the piston movement within the bore
Tillotson Carburettor manufacturer in the USA.
Torque induction An intake valve assembly and booster port arrangement designed to maintain the combustion efficiency of Yamaha 2-stroke engines at a peak under all operating conditions.
Transmission The function of the transmission is to transfer engine power to the driving wheel and in motorcycles this is normally achieved by primary and secondary chains and less commonly by shaft drive.
Triple A three-cylinder engine layout.
Twin Two-cylinder engine.
Vee-engine An engine arranged with its cylinders in a V shape.
Villiers British engine manufacturers, now part of NVT Group.
Zenith British carburettor manufacturer.

The Motorcycle – Then and Now

The motorcycle's ancestry is buried somewhere in the scatter of experiments with single-cylinder steam engines, crude 4-strokes and 'bone-shaker' bicycles at the end of the nineteenth century. Michaux and Perreaux in France, Daimler of Germany, Butler and Holden in Britain and the Paris-based Werner brothers who coined the name 'cyclemotor', can all be considered pioneers of the motorcycle. Certainly by 1894 Alois Wolfmüller and Hans Geisenhof had patented a 1 500 cc motorcycle capable of 40 km/h which was to be sold commercially in Germany and France. The subsequent 75-year history has seen a wealth of engineering experiment and the notes that follow give only the barest outline of the background to the complex machines of today. What cannot fail to impress is how often today's so-called innovations had already been tried out by original, pioneering motorcycle designers.

550 cc single-cylinder side-valve model H Triumph – 1915

Engines The first engines were generally single-cylinder, 4-stroke side-valves with air-cooling, simple carburettors and break-spark ignition from low-tension magnetos. Large, multi-cylinder engines, often vee-twins, soon appeared in an attempt to improve reliability and by World War I a whole range of engine types and layouts had appeared on the roads. During the 1920s monobloc designs became standard and the more efficient overhead-valve engines arrived with later overhead camshafts sometimes replacing push-rods and rockers. In the last thirty years the 2-stroke engine has been so perfected that it powers many of today's motorcycles although recent concern over pollution and their high fuel consumption has caused something of a swing back to the 4-stroke. Modern engines are as varied as ever with 2-strokes dominating the lightweight machines and multi-cylinder 4-strokes powering the superbikes. However, the rotary engine may be the power unit of the future.

Lubrication The first machines used hand-operated lubrication pumps but now bikes mostly use a pressurized oiling system like that used in cars; however some models have separate oil tanks to keep the lubricant cool. Significant changes have affected 2-strokes, which once needed a 20:1 petrol/oil mixture to prevent overheating and seizure, and suffered from plug oiling and excessive exhaust smoke. Modern lubricants have reduced the mixture ratio to 50:1 and patent oil injectors, such as Yamaha's Autolube and Suzuki's CCI, which involve separate, pressurized lubrication regulated by throttle action, have simplified the whole process.

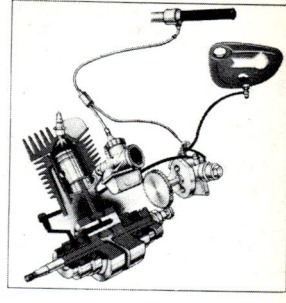

Suzuki CCI Lubrication

Dell'Orto slide carburettor

Carburettors Early motorcycles used surface vaporizers and wick-feed carburettors with separate float chamber, although the basic principle of the spray carburettor had appeared by 1902. Today the monobloc design with sliding piston throttle control is most common. Some bigger bikes have constant velocity carburettors with diaphragm control of the fuel/air mixture to achieve a gently progressive generation of engine power.

Starting Push starting soon gave way to kick-start devices. Surprisingly the electric starter has been available on motorcycles since 1914 when the Indian company used it on their vee-twin Hendee Special. Now it is beginning to become available on small bikes although it has required a switch to 12-volt electrics to provide sufficient power for the starter motor.

Ignition The flywheel magneto and high-tension coil were soon developed for the motorcycle and have remained a simple but practical form of electric system for most lightweight machines. Bigger bikes normally have a battery, generator (dynamo or alternator) and coil for ignition and lighting but the demands of modern, high-revving engines have benefited from the development of electronic ignition (CDI).

Transmission The simple, gearless, clutchless belt-transmission of the early motorcycles made them very inflexible in use and the success of the 1911 2-speed Indian models over the newly opened mountain course of the Isle of Man proved the value of the gearbox and chain drive. Most bikes now have 4-, 5- and even 6-speed gearboxes with multi-plate clutches in an oil bath. The original hand-operated gear levers were altered to foot control in the 1930s, and only recently the gear change position has been standardized on the US/Japanese pattern. Belt final-drive slipped badly and soon gave way to the roller chain. Shaft drive, as used in cars, is still only found on a few luxury bikes although it was first used as long ago as 1905 by the Belgian FN company. Automatic transmission, using a centrifugal clutch and variable-belt drive, is common on mopeds and there are scooters with direct transmission to the rear wheel. The Moto Guzzi V1000 provides a unique example of automatic drive via a car-type hydraulic torque converter and two-speed gearbox.

Frame/Suspension The bicycle frames of early motorcycles lacked stability and strength and today's machines are mostly built around a heavy-duty steel frame in a continuous double cradle. For commuter bikes the 'step-thru' has become very popular as a compromise between the monocoque body of the scooter and the motorcycle with working parts exposed. Vibration has long been a problem in motorcycles and the Norton 'Isolastic' mounting system is an original solution, effectively insulating the engine from the frame. Isolation is achieved by the use of resilient mountings at A, B and C.

Norton anti-vibration Isolastic system

Until World War II front-wheel suspension was commonly of the girder type with spiral springing, even though the telescopic forks which are standard practice today had been developed early on. The leading link form of front suspension is usually only found now on scooters and certain lightweights. Early machines used a variety of rear springing from leaf springs to air springs, but rear suspension was not generally improved until the late 1930s. The swinging arm cushioned by adjustable hydraulic dampers, which is today's universal solution, appeared widely after World War II. Some trail bikes are now fitted with cantilever-type monoshock suspension with dampers using oil and inert gas.

The 350 cc twin-cylinder, torque induction 2-stroke Yamaha 1975 illustrates the characteristics of modern motorcycles

Brakes The original motorcycle brakes were copied from bicycles, and there are still some mopeds that use rim calipers. The more efficient internal expanding drum brakes have been a standard feature since the 1920s but in the last few years the hydraulic disc brake has become popular, at first only on the front wheel, but latterly on both wheels. The massive stopping power of these large discs has led one superbike manufacturer to fit coupled brakes protected by a rear-brake load-limiter. The perforated discs fitted to some bikes are designed to prevent the formation of a water film in wet weather, which delays the braking effect.

Double disc as fitted to BMW bikes

Tyres Spoked wheels are still standard fittings to most motorcycles although the use of magnesium alloy wheels in racing is likely to spread

Magnesium wheels on KTM 50RS

to production models. Better roads and suspension improvements have tended to result in smaller wheels, although trials machines still have the large wheels to help the rider negotiate rough surfaces. As with motor-car tyres, the experiments with tread design and rubber compound for high-speed road-racing have led to substantial improvements in the tyres available to the ordinary motorcyclist.

Lighting Until the 1920s acetylene lighting was common on motorcycles although Indian bikes had been fitted with electric lamps by 1914. Smaller bikes and mopeds still normally have 6-volt magneto lighting and, therefore, they are lit only while the engine is running, but the use of alternators and large-capacity 12-volt batteries has improved the whole electrical system of motorcycles which for a long time had been a weakness in design. Fast superbike tourers need good illumination for night-riding and modern machines are now fitted with large-diameter quartz halogen headlamps with directed beam, car-type flashing indicators and instrument panels containing tell-tale lights for neutral, oil pressure, brake fluid, main beam and turn.

BMWR 90S instrument panel

Craven Comet Panniers and Spaceman Top Case

Accessories Motorcyclists, like car owners, have always enjoyed customizing their machines both to improve performance and appearance. Fibreglass has tended to replace the leather and metal accessories of the early days and the possibilities of the full treatment can be seen in the example of the Paul Dunstall version of the Kawasaki 900 on the opposite page.

Sidecars A comparative rarity today, although throughout the 1920s and 1930s the sidecar was an extremely popular form of cheap transport.

Dunstall Kawasaki 900 fitted with clip-ons, power exhaust, decibel silencers, rear-seat footrest, tank-seat assembly and glass-fibre mudguard.

985 cc vee-twin side-valve BSA and sidecar – 1922 (Crown Copyright. Science Museum, London)

Specialist Motorcycles

Apart from its roles as a cheap form of personal transport and a source of leisure entertainment, the virtues of the motorcycle have long been recognized by the police and armed forces. In both world wars motorcycles were widely used for communication and reconnaissance work and most armed forces include them amongst their tactical transport vehicles. They are normally domestically produced machines modified with heavy-duty components and fitted with carriers.

BSA B40 Mk 1 & 3. 343 cc single, 4-speed developing 18 bhp and 88 km/h. Manufactured by BSA Co Ltd, Small Heath, Birmingham, England, for the British army.

Condor A350, 340 cc single, 5-speed developing 16.6 bhp and 120 km/h. Manufactured by Condor SA, Courfaire BE, Switzerland, for Swiss armed forces.

Police forces around the world use powerful motorcycles for traffic-control duties. The modifications normally made include the fitting of multi-channel radios, air horns, flashing lights and sirens, and full fairings.

Metropolitan Police Traffic Division use 340 of these Triumph TR6.

West Midlands Police Traffic Division use 100 of these Norton 'Interpol'.

Motorcycles are also frequently used for special delivery work where mobility and reliability are essential requirements. Thus motorcycles are used for emergency delivery of drugs and other medical supplies, the transport of computer data and business letters around crowded city centres and the rush collection of television film and news items. In some countries, in three-wheel form, the motorcycle has even wider transportation uses, carrying passengers and freight simply and economically.

AJW (UK)

Wolfhound

Engine:
Type 2-str Minarelli single
Bore × Stroke 38.8 × 42 mm
Capacity 49.7 cc
Compression ratio 12:1
Carburettors 1/19 mm Dell'Orto
Maximum power 6.0 @ 9 000
Fuel tank 10 l

Transmission:
Gears/Clutch 6/wmp

Electrical:
Ignition 6 v/magneto
Starting Kick or pedal

Notes: 80 cc version available.

Braking:
Front/Rear 118 mm drums
Front tyres 2.50 × 19 trials
Rear tyres 3.00 × 17 trials

Suspension:
Front/Rear T/SA

Dimensions:
Ground clearance 230 mm
Seat height 750 mm
Wheelbase 1 200 mm
Overall length 1 900 mm
Dry weight 68 kg

Performance:
Top speed 80 km/h
Fuel consumption 3 l/100 km

AJW

Greyhound

Engine:
Type 2-str Minarelli single
Bore × Stroke 38.8 × 42 mm
Capacity 49.7 cc
Compression ratio 12:1
Carburettors 1/19 mm Dell'Orto
Maximum power 4.5 @ 9 000
Fuel tank 10 l

Transmission:
Gears/Clutch 6/wmp

Electrical:
Ignition 6 v/magneto
Starting Kick or pedal

Notes:

Braking:
Front/Rear 118 mm drums
Front tyres 2.50 × 17 road
Rear tyres 2.75 × 17 road

Suspension:
Front/Rear T/SA

Dimensions:
Ground clearance 145 mm
Seat height 720 mm
Wheelbase 1 120 mm
Overall length 1 740 mm
Dry weight 66 kg

Performance:
Top speed 80 km/h
Fuel consumption 3 l/100 km

AJW

Pointer

Engine:
Type 2-str horizontal single
Bore × Stroke 38.8 × 42 mm
Capacity 49.7 cc
Compression ratio 12:1
Carburettors 1/12 mm Dell'Orto
Maximum power 1.7 @ 6 500
Fuel tank 3.5 l

Transmission:
Gears/Clutch single/automatic

Electrical:
Ignition 6 v/magneto
Starting pedal

Notes:

Braking:
Front/Rear 105 mm drums
Front tyres 2.25 × 16 road
Rear tyres 2.25 × 16 road

Suspension:
Front/Rear T/SA

Dimensions:
Ground clearance 165 mm
Seat height 800 mm
Wheelbase 1 045 mm
Overall length 1 610 mm
Dry weight 46 kg

Performance:
Top speed 56 km/h
Fuel consumption 2.5 l/100 km

AJW   Collie

Engine:
Type 2-str Minarelli single
Bore × Stroke 38.8 × 42 mm
Capacity 47.6 cc
Compression ratio ...
Carburettors 1/14 mm Dell'Orto
Maximum power 3.5 @ 6 500
Fuel tank 5 l

Transmission:
Gears/Clutch 3/wmp

Electrical:
Ignition 6 v/magneto
Starting kick or pedal

Notes: Collie is a goods moped with a payload of 86 kg.

Braking:
Front/Rear 105 mm drums
Front tyres 3.00 × 12 road
Rear tyres 3.00 × 12 road

Suspension:
Front/Rear LL/SA

Dimensions:
Ground clearance 135 mm
Seat height 800 mm
Wheelbase 980 mm
Overall length 1 610 mm
Dry weight 70 kg

Performance:
Top speed 56 km/h
Fuel consumption 2.8 l/100 km

 AJW Motorcycles Ltd is a small British manufacturer, founded by Arthur John Wheaton, an Exeter printer, in 1926 and has been under the same family management since 1946. The firm originally used J.A.P. engines and in 1928 produced a water-cooled 985 cc Super Four with a completely enclosed steel chassis. The Exeter plant was bombed in 1940 and operations were then switched to Wimborne, Dorset. Although the 500 cc Fox models were continued until the fifties, after 1957 production concentrated on Minarelli-engined mopeds and lightweights. Now a wide range of 50 cc and 80 cc machines are built in Italy by Peripoli Fratelli S.n.c. to AJW designs and specifications. Other models include the Airedale, a 3-speed moped with step-thru frame and the Whippet which develops 3.5 uhp from the 47.6 cc engine.
Head Office: AJW Motorcycles Ltd, Crowvale Depot, Stone Close, Horton Road, West Drayton, Middx, England.
Technical & Design: Pilford Heath, Wimborne, Dorset, BH21 2LW.

Bajaj (India) Chetak

Engine:
Type 2-str rotary valve single
Bore × Stroke   57 × 57 mm
Capacity   145.45 cc
Compression ratio   7.4:1
Carburettors   1/18 mm Dell'Orto
Maximum power   6.3 @ 5 200
Fuel tank   7.7 l

Transmission:
Gears   4/constant mesh

Electrical:
Ignition   6 v/magneto
Starting   kick

Notes: †Helical springs and double-acting hydraulic shock absorbers.

Braking:
Front/Rear   150 mm drums
Front tyres   3.50 × 10 road
Rear tyres   3.50 × 10 road

Suspension:
Front/Rear   †

Dimensions:
Ground clearance   130 mm
Seat height   787 mm
Wheelbase   1 200 mm
Overall length   1 770 mm
Dry weight   96 kg

Performance:
Top speed   90 km/h
Fuel consumption   2.5 l/100 km

bajaj auto ltd was formed in 1945 and today produces some 55 000 scooters and 8 000 three-wheeled autorickshaws and delivery vans a year from a modern factory 150 km east of Bombay. Prior to 1971 Bajaj scooters were assembled under licence from Piaggio of Italy, using imported components, but since then manufacture has become almost completely domestic. The company now markets two scooter models, a basic 150 cc Vespa design and the Chetak which features additionally a more powerful engine and 4-speed gearbox.
Head Office: bajaj auto limited, Bombay Poona Road, Akurdi, Poona – 411035 (India).

Batavus (The Netherlands)   MK 4S

Engine:
Type 2-str Sachs single
Bore × Stroke 38 × 42 mm
Capacity 47 cc
Compression ratio 9:1
Carburettors 1/18 mm Bing
Maximum power 3 @ 6 000
Fuel tank 11 l

Transmission:
Gears/Clutch 4/wmp

Electrical:
Ignition 6 v/4 Ah/magneto
Starting pedal

Notes:

Braking:
Front/Rear 127 mm drums
Front tyres 2.25 × 17 road
Rear tyres 2.25 × 17 road

Suspension:
Front/Rear T/SA

Dimensions:
Ground clearance 180 mm
Seat height 736 mm
Wheelbase 1 170 mm
Overall length 1 879 mm
Dry weight 65 kg

Performance:
Top speed 80 km/h
Fuel consumption 2 l/100 km

BATAVUS

Batavus is the main Dutch moped and bicycle manufacturer in a country which has over 2 million mopeds on the roads. The company employs a labour force of about 650 in a modern factory using advanced design and manufacturing techniques. The HS 50 was built by Batavus to a Harglo specification for the British market and the success of the design has resulted in its now being sold in several of the Common Market countries including the Netherlands.

Head Office: Batavus Intercycle B.V., Industrieweg 4, P.O.B. 515, Heerenveen, The Netherlands.
UK Concessionaires: Harglo Ltd, 462 Station Road, Dorridge, Solihull, Warwicks.

Batavus   **HS 50**

Engine:
Type 2-str reed valve single
Bore × Stroke 40 × 38 mm
Capacity 48 cc
Compression ratio 7 : 1
Carburettors 1/12 mm Encarwi
Maximum power 2.4 @ 5 000
Fuel tank 3.5 l

Transmission:
Gears/Clutch single/A

Electrical:
Ignition 6 v/magneto
Starting pedal

Notes: Laura, Bronco and Go-Go models are similar specification. Compact has 3.00 × 10 wheels.

Braking:
Front/Rear 80 mm dm/70 mm dm
Front tyres 2.00 × 16 road
Rear tyres 2.00 × 16 road

Suspension:
Front/Rear T/SA

Dimensions:
Ground clearance 160 mm
Seat height 711 mm
Wheelbase 1 080 mm
Overall length 1 625 mm
Dry weight 39 kg

Performance:
Top speed 62 km/h
Fuel consumption 1.7 l/100 km

Batavus Compact

Benelli (Italy)

750 Sei

Engine:
Type 4-str sohc six
Bore×Stroke 56×50.6 mm
Capacity 747.77 cc
Compression ratio 9.8 : 1
Carburettors 3/24 mm Dell'Orto
Maximum power 71 @ 8 900*
Fuel tank 23 l

Transmission:
Gears/Clutch 5/wmp

Electrical:
Ignition 12 v/15 Ah/b&c/A
Starting electric

Notes:

Braking:
Front/Rear 300 mm dc/200 mm dc
Front tyres 3.50×18 road
Rear tyres 4.10×18 road

Suspension:
Front/Rear T/SA

Dimensions:
Ground clearance 140 mm
Seat height 800 mm
Wheelbase 1 430 mm
Overall length 2 120 mm
Dry weight 220 kg

Performance:
Top speed 194 km/h
Fuel consumption 6.2 l/100 km (p)

Benelli 500 Quattro

Engine:
Type 4-str ohc four
Bore×Stroke 56×50.6 mm
Capacity 498 cc
Compression ratio 10.2 : 1
Carburettors 4/22 mm Dell'Orto
Maximum power ...
Fuel tank 23 l

Transmission:
Gears/Clutch 5/wmp

Electrical:
Ignition 12 v/b&c/D
Starting electric

Notes: Also available in 650 form developing 50 bhp @ 7 000 rpm

Braking:
Front/Rear 300 mm dm/200 mm dm
Front tyres 3.50×18 road
Rear tyres 4.00×18 road

Suspension:
Front/Rear T/SA (3-pos.)

Dimensions:
Ground clearance 165 mm
Seat height 787 mm
Wheelbase 1 422 mm
Overall length 2 100 mm
Dry weight 209 kg

Performance:
Top speed ...
Fuel consumption 4.6 l/100 km (p)

Benelli 250 2c

Engine:
Type 2-str vertical twin
Bore×Stroke 56×47 mm
Capacity 231.3 cc
Compression ratio 10 : 1
Carburettors 2/22 mm Dell'Orto
Maximum power 25 @ 6 850
Fuel tank 14 l

Transmission:
Gears/Clutch 5/wmp

Electrical:
Ignition 6 v/9 Ah/ε/A
Starting kick

Notes: Also in 125 cc version developing 15.4 bhp @ 7 750.

Braking:
Front/Rear 180 mm dm/160 mm dm
Front tyres 3.00×18 road
Rear tyres 3.25×18 road

Suspension:
Front/Rear T/SA (3-pos.)

Dimensions:
Ground clearance 165 mm
Seat height 800 mm
Wheelbase 1 310 mm
Overall length 1 950 mm
Dry weight 134 kg

Performance:
Top speed 145 km/h
Fuel consumption 4.4 l/100 km

Benelli   **125 Cross**

Engine:
Type 2-str single
Bore × Stroke 56 × 49 mm
Capacity 124.77 cc
Compression ratio 9.5 : 1
Carburettors 1/22 mm Dell'Orto
Maximum power 14 @ 6 500
Fuel tank 9 l

Transmission:
Gears/Clutch 5/wmp

Electrical:
Ignition 6 v/8 Ah/magneto
Starting kick

Notes:

Braking:
Front/Rear 135 mm drums
Front tyres 2.50 × 21 trials
Rear tyres 3.50 × 18 trials

Suspension:
Front/Rear T/SA (3-pos.)

Dimensions:
Ground clearance 280 mm
Seat height 800 mm
Wheelbase 1 285 mm
Overall length 1 970 mm
Dry weight 98 kg

Performance:
Top speed 105 km/h
Fuel consumption 4 l/100 km

Benelli   The house of Benelli was founded in 1911 by five Benelli brothers to manufacture motorcycles and parts. During the fifties the manufacture of 49 cc mopeds and 50 cc lightweights was run independently by one of the Benelli brothers under the Motobi label but this became part of the main organization in 1962. The Benelli factory was destroyed during World War II and the present plant with its workforce of 750 employees is now part of the De Tomaso group which also owns Moto Guzzi. Benelli has been closely associated with road racing since the mid-twenties and has several times won the 250 cc world championship. The unique 750 Sei is the only 6-cylinder motorcycle made in the world and is in startling contrast to the 49 cc moped models also made by the company.
Head Office: Fratelli Benelli S.p.A., 61100 Pesaro – viale Mameli 22, Italy.
UK Concessionaires: Agrati Sales (UK) Ltd, St Mark's Street, Nottingham NG3 1DA.

Betamotor (Italy)

Betamotor started manufacturing cycles in 1904 and only since the fifties has it made engines, mopeds and motorcycles. Its range includes the single-speed Holly moped, the 3-speed Pullman and the 4-speed Camoscio. The 4-speed Boy Special has a similar specification to the Bambi and both models under Italian law are defined as light motorcycles and may be ridden by fourteen-year-olds.

Head Office: Betamotor S.p.A., 50145 Firenze (Brozzi), Italy.

Beta

Engine:
Type   2-str single
Bore × Stroke   70 × 64.5 mm
Capacity   248 cc
Compression ratio   12.5 : 1
Carburettors   1/36 mm Dell'Orto
Maximum power   30 @ 7500
Fuel tank   10 l

Transmission:
Gears/Clutch   5/wmp

Electrical:
Ignition   6 v/c/magneto
Starting   kick

Notes: 48 cc, 125 cc trial models also available.

CR 250 (Trial)

Braking:
Front/Rear   140 mm dm/160 mm dm
Front tyres   3.00 × 21 trials
Rear tyres   4.00 × 18 trials

Suspension:
Front/Rear   T/SA

Dimensions:
Ground clearance   …
Seat height   …
Wheelbase   …
Overall length   …
Dry weight   112 kg

Performance:
Top speed   125 km/h
Fuel consumption   7 l/100 km

Beta   **Bambi**

Engine:
Type   2-str horizontal single
Bore×Stroke   40×39 mm
Capacity   49 cc
Compression ratio   8.5:1
Carburettors   1/14 mm Dell'Orto
Maximum power   under 1.5 hp
Fuel tank   3 l

Transmission:
Gears/Clutch   single/A

Electrical:
Ignition   6 v/magneto
Starting   kick

Notes:

Braking:
Front/Rear   90 mm drums
Front tyres   3.00×10 road
Rear tyres   3.00×10 road

Suspension:
Front/Rear   T/SA

Dimensions:
Ground clearance   ...
Seat height   ...
Wheelbase   ...
Overall length   ...
Dry weight   46 kg

Performance:
Top speed   40 km/h
Fuel consumption   2.5 l/100 km

**Betamotor
Boy Special**

BMW (West Germany)

Over fifty years of well-tried tradition with constant modernization and design development result in BMW producing powerful and comfortable machines which are outstanding examples of motorcycle engineering. The basic concept of a transversely mounted, horizontally opposed engine with shaft drive designed by Dr Ing. Max Friz has remained unchanged since the 500 cc R32 model appeared at the Paris Motor Show in 1923.

The Bayerische Motoren Werke at Munich was founded in 1917 for the manufacture of aero engines, and motorcycle production did not begin until the 1920s. Although the BMW reputation is based on the flat-twin the company has built many single-cylinder models particularly after World War II when German manufacturers were obliged to make motorcycles of 250 cc or less. The R27, a 250 cc ohv single was produced until 1967. Today the large, luxury twins complement the company's high-performance motor cars and are widely used for police duties.

BMW has pioneered a number of technical innovations in motorcycle design, including its constant use of shaft drive, the first use of hydraulically damped telescopic forks in 1935, the introduction of twin leading-shoe drum brakes in the fifties, the first use of perforated disc brakes on production bikes and the relegation of the kick starter to an optional extra. Top of its present range is the R90S, a high-performance machine with four-instrument cockpit and there is also the R90/6 which is similar to the R75/6 but has the bigger 898 cc engine developing 60 bhp and a top speed of 180 km/h. In the 1930s BMW bikes held many world speed records and since 1954 have dominated the world side-car racing championship.

Head Office: BMW Motorrad GmbH, 8 München 40, Volckerstrasse 9, West Germany.
UK Concessionaires: BMW (GB) Ltd, 991 Great West Road, Brentford, TW8 9ED.

BMW R32 500 cc side valve developing 8.5 bhp @ 3 300 rpm and made between 1923/26

BMW R90S

Engine:
Type 4-str ohv flat twin
Bore × Stroke 90 × 70.6 mm
Capacity 898 cc
Compression ratio 9.5 : 1
Carburettors 2/38 mm Dell'Orto
Maximum power 67 @ 7 000
Fuel tank 24 l

Transmission:
Gears/Clutch 5/dsp

Electrical:
Ignition 12v/25 Ah/b&c/A
Starting electric

Notes:

Braking:
Front/Rear 260 mm dc/200 mm dm
Front tyres 3.25 × 19 road
Rear tyres 4.00 × 18 road

Suspension:
Front/Rear T/SA (3-pos.)

Dimensions:
Ground clearance 165 mm
Seat height 820 mm
Wheelbase 1 465 mm
Overall length 2 180 mm
Dry weight 190 kg

Performance:
Top speed 195 km/h
Fuel consumption 5 l/100 km

BMW R75/6

Engine:
Type 4-str ohv flat twin
Bore × stroke 82 × 70.6 mm
Capacity 745 cc
Compression ratio 9:1
Carburettors 2/32 mm Bing
Maximum power 50 @ 6 200
Fuel tank 18 l

Transmission:
Gears/Clutch 5/dsp

Electrical:
Ignition 12 v/25 Ah/b&c/A
Starting electric

Notes: Available as R90/6 with 898 cc engine.

Braking:
Front/Rear 260 mm dc/200 mm dm
Front tyres 3.25 × 19 road
Rear tyres 4.00 × 18 road

Suspension:
Front/Rear T/SA (3-pos.)

Dimensions:
Ground clearance 165 mm
Seat height 810 mm
Wheelbase 1 465 mm
Overall length 2 180 mm
Dry weight 190 kg

Performance:
Top speed 170 km/h
Fuel consumption 4.6 l/100 km

BMW R60/6

Engine:
Type 4-str ohv flat twin
Bore × Stroke 73.5 × 70.6 mm
Capacity 599 cc
Compression ratio 9.2 : 1
Carburettors 2/26 mm Bing
Maximum power 40 @ 6 400
Fuel tank 18 l

Transmission:
Gears/Clutch 5/dsp

Electrical:
Ignition 12 v/25 Ah/b&c/A
Starting electric

Notes:

Braking:
Front/Rear 200 mm drums
Front tyres 3.25 × 19 road
Rear tyres 4.00 × 19 road

Suspension:
Front/Rear T/SA (3-pos.)

Dimensions:
Ground clearance 165 mm
Seat height 810 mm
Wheelbase 1 465 mm
Overall length 2 180 mm
Dry weight 190 kg

Performance:
Top speed 160 km/h
Fuel consumption 4.8 l/180 km

Bultaco (Spain)

Engine:
Type 2-str single
Bore×Stroke 85×64 mm
Capacity 363.168 cc
Compression ratio 10:1
Carburettors 1/36 mm Amal
Maximum power 36 @ 7 000
Fuel tank 17 l

Transmission:
Gears/Clutch 5/wmp

Electrical:
Ignition 6 v/magneto
Starting kick

Notes:

Montjuic (141)

Braking:
Front/Rear 230 mm dm/160 mm dm
Front tyres 3.25×19 road
Rear tyres 4.00×18 road

Suspension:
Front/Rear T/SA

Dimensions:
Ground clearance 120 mm
Seat height 800 mm
Wheelbase 1 330 mm
Overall length 1 980 mm
Dry weight 135 kg

Performance:
Top speed 180 km/h
Fuel consumption ...

Bultaco

Engine:
Type 2-str single
Bore×Stroke 72×60 mm
Capacity 244.29 cc
Compression ratio 10:1
Carburettors 1/32 mm Amal
Maximum power 23 @ 7 500
Fuel tank 13 l

Transmission:
Gears/Clutch 5/wmp

Electrical:
Ignition 6 v/magneto
Starting kick

Notes: Also available with electric start (model 154).

Metralla GT (142)

Braking:
Front/Rear 160 mm drums
Front tyres 3.25×19 road
Rear tyres 3.50×18 road

Suspension:
Front/Rear T/SA

Dimensions:
Ground clearance 195 mm
Seat height 775 mm
Wheelbase 1 345 mm
Overall length 2 050 mm
Dry weight 118 kg

Performance:
Top speed 145 km/h
Fuel consumption ...

Bultaco

Engine:
Type 2-str single
Bore×Stroke 56×60 mm
Capacity 147.8 cc
Compression ratio 7.7:1
Carburettors 1/20 mm Zenith
Maximum power 8.05 @ 5 500
Fuel tank 11.5 l

Transmission:
Gears/Clutch 5/wmp

Electrical:
Ignition 6 v/magneto
Starting kick

Notes:

Mercurio GT (139)

Braking:
Front/Rear 140 mm drums
Front tyres 3.00×17 road
Rear tyres 3.00×17 road

Suspension:
Front/Rear T/SA

Dimensions:
Ground clearance ...
Seat height 760 mm
Wheelbase 1 270 mm
Overall length 1915 mm
Dry weight 95 kg

Performance:
Top speed 100 km/h
Fuel consumption 2 l/100 km

Bultaco   **Junior GT2 (130)**

Engine:
Type   2-str single
Bore × Stroke   43 × 51.5 mm
Capacity   74.78 cc
Compression ratio   9 : 1
Carburettors   1/18 mm Zenith
Maximum power   7 @ 7 000
Fuel tank   7.6 l

Transmission:
Gears/Clutch   4/wmp

Electrical:
Ignition   6 v/magneto
Starting   kick

Notes: Also with 125 cc engine developing 12.5 bhp. Model (131).

Braking:
Front/Rear   125 mm drums
Front tyres   2.50 × 17 road
Rear tyres   2.50 × 17 road

Suspension:
Front/Rear   T/SA

Dimensions:
Ground clearance   210 mm
Seat height   730 mm
Wheelbase   1 215 mm
Overall length   1 800 mm
Dry weight   77 kg

Performance:
Top speed   …
Fuel consumption   …

The Spanish Bultaco works were started in 1958 by the ex-Montesa designer Francesco Bulto when Montesa decided to withdraw from grand prix racing. The new company commenced operations from a farmhouse near Barcelona but soon established a world reputation in all forms of two-wheeled sport, particularly in moto-cross and ISDT competitions. In addition to the road bikes sold mainly on the home market, Bultaco export a wide range of enduro and trials machines such as the 5-speed Frontera, Pursang and Sherpa models.
Head Office: Bultaco Compañia Española de Motores, S.A., Mas Casellas–La Catalana, San Adrian de Besos (Barcelona), Spain.
UK Concessionaires: Comerfords Ltd, Portsmouth Road, Thames Ditton, Surrey KT7 OXQ.

Casal (Portugal)

Metalurgia Casal, the best-known Portuguese motorcycle manufacturer, started as a family firm in 1953 and at first made agricultural and industrial engines as well as engines for motorcycles. Its first two-wheeler was the Carina scooter but since then the range has widened to include mopeds and motorcycles up to 250 cc. Casal motorcycles are exported from a modern, well-equipped factory, some 60 km south of Porto, to Scandinavian countries, the UK, France, West Germany, Greece, Iran, Australia, Venezuela, the USA and several African states.

Head Office: Metalurgia Casal S.A.R.L., PO Box 83, Aveiro, Portugal.
UK Concessionaires: Alan Taylor (Northern) Ltd, Elan House, Manchester Road, Castleton, Rochdale, Lancashire OL11 2XY.

Casal K272

Engine:
Type 2-str single
Bore × Stroke 58 × 54 mm
Capacity 142.6 cc
Compression ratio 8.5:1
Carburettors 1/Bing
Maximum power 15 @ 7 500
Fuel tank 12 l

Transmission:
Gears/Clutch 5/wmp

Electrical:
Ignition 6 v/b/magneto
Starting Kick

Notes: K280 250 cc and K270 125 cc models also available.

Braking:
Front/Rear 160 mm drums
Front tyres 3.00 × 18 road
Rear tyres 3.25 × 18 road

Suspension:
Front/Rear T/SA (3-pos.)

Dimensions:
Ground clearance 210 mm
Seat height 810 mm
Wheelbase ...
Overall length 1 980 mm
Dry weight 120 kg

Performance:
Top speed 130 km/h
Fuel consumption 3.5 l/100 km

Casal SS4

Engine:
Type 2-str single
Bore × Stroke 40 × 39.7 mm
Capacity 49.9 cc
Compression ratio 8.5:1
Carburettors 1/19 mm Bing
Maximum power 5.3 @ 7 500
Fuel tank 8 l

Transmission:
Gears/Clutch 4/wmp

Electrical:
Ignition 6 v/b/magneto
Starting pedal

Notes: SS5 is a 5-speed version and ST50 is a trials model.

Braking:
Front/Rear 140 mm drums
Front tyres 2.75 × 21 road
Rear tyres 2.75 × 21 road

Suspension:
Front/Rear T/SA

Dimensions:
Ground clearance 180 mm
Seat height 830 mm
Wheelbase 1219 mm
Overall length 1810 mm
Dry weight 68 kg

Performance:
Top speed 90 km/h
Fuel consumption 3.1 l/100 km

Casal S2

Engine:
Type 2-str single
Bore × Stroke 40 × 39.7 mm
Capacity 49.9 cc
Compression ratio 8.5:1
Carburettors 1/19 mm Bing
Maximum power 2.5 @ 5 500

Transmission:
Gears/Clutch 2/wmp

Electrical:
Ignition 6 v/magneto
Starting pedal

Notes:

Braking:
Front/Rear 120 mm drums
Front tyres 2.25 × 20 road
Rear tyres 2.25 × 20 road

Suspension:
Front/Rear T/SA

Dimensions:
Ground clearance 180 mm
Seat height 830 mm
Wheelbase 1 219 mm
Overall length 1810 mm
Dry weight 58 kg

Performance:
Top speed 55 km/h
Fuel consumption 2.2 l/100 km

Casal K 168 Boss

Engine:
Type 2-str single
Bore × Stroke 40 × 39.7 mm
Capacity 49.9 cc
Compression ratio 8.5:1
Carburettors 1/19 mm Bing
Maximum power 2.5 @ 5 500
Fuel tank 4 l

Transmission:
Gears/Clutch 2/wmp

Electrical:
Ignition 6 v/magneto
Starting pedal

Notes: K165 Mirabelle automatic moped also available.

Braking:
Front/Rear 120 mm drums
Front tyres 2.25 × 20 road
Rear ryres 2.25 × 20 road

Suspension:
Front/Rear T/SA

Dimensions:
Ground clearance ...
Seat height 830 mm
Wheelbase 1 200 mm
Overall length 1 755 mm
Dry weight 55 kg

Performance:
Top speed 55 km/h
Fuel consumption 2.2 l/100 km

Cimatti (Italy)

Engine:
Type 2-str single
Bore × Stroke 38.8 × 42 mm
Capacity 49.6 cc
Compression ratio 11.5 : 1
Carburettors 1/19 mm Dell'Orto
Maximum power 6.5 @ 8 500
Fuel tank 9 l

Transmission:
Gears/Clutch 6/wmp

Electrical:
Ignition 6 v/magneto
Starting pedal

Notes:

Cimatti

Engine:
Type 2-str single
Bore × Stroke 38 × 42 mm
Capacity 49.6 cc
Compression ratio 11.5 : 1
Carburettors 1/19 mm Dell'Orto
Maximum power 6.5 @ 8 500
Fuel tank 8 l

Transmission:
Gears/Clutch 6/wmp

Electrical:
Ignition 6 v/magneto
Starting pedal

Notes: 125 cc version available.

Cimatti

Engine:
Type 2-str single
Bore × Stroke 39 × 41.8 mm
Capacity 49 cc
Compression ratio 9 : 1
Carburettors 1/19 mm Dell'Orto
Maximum power 6.0 @ 8 000
Fuel tank 4.1 l

Transmission:
Gears/Clutch 4/wmp

Electrical:
Ignition 6 v/magneto
Starting pedal

Notes: Uses Moto Morini engine

Sagittario

Braking:
Front/Rear 118 mm dm/105 mm dm
Front tyres 2.25 × 18 road
Rear tyres 2.25 × 18 road

Suspension:
Front/Rear T/SA

Dimensions:
Ground clearance 210 mm
Seat height 720 mm
Wheelbase 1 140 mm
Overall length 1 730 mm
Dry weight 62 kg

Performance:
Top speed 80 km/h
Fuel consumption 2.1 l/100 km

Kaiman Trail

Braking:
Front/Rear 118 mm drums
Front tyres 2.50 × 19 trials
Rear tyres 3.00 × 17 trials

Suspension:
Front/Rear T/SA

Dimensions:
Ground clearance 250 mm
Seat height 750 mm
Wheelbase 1 240 mm
Overall length 1 835 mm
Dry weight 71 kg

Performance:
Top speed 80 km/h
Fuel consumption ...

Bob-Cat Fun Bike

Braking:
Front/Rear 105 mm drums
Front tyres 4.00 × 10 road
Rear tyres 4.00 × 10 road

Suspension:
Front/Rear T/SA

Dimensions:
Ground clearance 60 mm
Seat height 700 mm
Wheelbase 1 040 mm
Overall length 1 500 mm
Dry weight 59 kg

Performance:
Top speed 75 km/h
Fuel consumption 1.8 l/100 km

Cimatti — Chic

Engine:
Type 2-str horizontal single
Bore × Stroke 38.8 × 42 mm
Capacity 49.6 cc
Compression ratio 8:1
Carburettors 1/14 mm Dell'Orto
Maximum power 1.9 @ 4 800
Fuel tank 3.5 l

Transmission:
Gears/Clutch single/A

Electrical:
Ignition 6 v/magneto
Starting pedal

Notes: Also in Mini Chic version with 3.00 × 10 tyres and a variable speed model.

Braking:
Front/Rear 102 mm drums
Front tyres 2.25 × 16 road
Rear tyres 2.25 × 16 road

Suspension:
Front/Rear T/SA

Dimensions:
Ground clearance 100 mm
Seat height 788–930 mm
Wheelbase 1 060 mm
Overall length 1 620 mm
Dry weight 45 kg

Performance:
Top speed 64 km/h
Fuel consumption 1.5 l/100 km

Cimatti mopeds and lightweight motorcycles use Moto Minarelli engines and are designed and manufactured in Bologna, Italy. The range also includes the Piper and Clan step-thru models and the recently introduced 125 cc Ariete. The Piper comes in automatic and 4-speed versions with fuel-carrying frames and strong luggage carriers. Cimatti also manufactures bicycles.
Head Office: Cimatti Enrico S.p.A., 40040 Pioppe Di Salvaro, Grizzano (Bologna), Italy.
UK Concessionaires: Anderson Motors Ltd, 31–3 Buxton Road, Hazel Grove, Stockport, Cheshire SK7 6AQ.

Cossack (USSR)

Dneiper

Engine:
Type 4-str horizontally opp. twin
Bore × Stroke 78 × 68 mm
Capacity 649 cc
Compression ratio 7:1
Carburettors 2/24 mm
Maximum power 32 @ 5 200
Fuel tank 18 l

Transmission:
Gears/Clutch 4/2 dp

Electrical:
Ignition 6 v/14 Ah/b&c/D
Starting kick

Notes: Single-seat side-car available with spare wheel and reverse gear.

Braking:
Front/Rear 202 mm drums
Front tyres 3.75 × 19 road
Rear tyres 3.75 × 19 road

Suspension:
Front/Rear T/SA

Dimensions:
Ground clearance 165 mm
Seat height 845 mm
Wheelbase 1 420 mm
Overall length 2 140 mm
Dry weight 210 kg

Performance:
Top speed 136 km/h
Fuel consumption 4.8 l/100 km

Cossack motorcycles are imported from the USSR by the Satra Corporation, an American trading organization, which holds exclusive marketing rights for sales of Soviet cars, motorcycles, bicycles, farm equipment and industrial machinery in North America, the UK and West Germany. Russian motorcycle factories tend to specialize in one model production, and the Cossack range which also includes the 650 cc horizontally opposed 4-stroke Ural and the 350 cc Jupiter twin are assembled at several locations in the Soviet Union including Minsk, Izhevsk and Kiev. These bikes are designed and equipped for easy owner-maintenance and their availability as combination outfits ex-factory is unique when side-cars have become something of a rarity.

UK Concessionaires: Satra Belarus Ltd, Motorcycle Division, Canada Road, Oyster Lane, Byfleet, Surrey KT14 7J.

Cossack

Engine:
Type 2-str single
Bore×Stroke 76×75 mm
Capacity 340 cc
Compression ratio 10:1
Carburettors 1/Mikuni
Maximum power 32 @ 6 000*
Fuel tank 18.2 l

Transmission:
Gears/Clutch 4/wmp

Electrical:
Ignition 12 v/b&c/D
Starting kick

Notes: First Soviet-built bike with direct positive oiling.

Cossack

Engine:
Type 2-str single
Bore×Stroke 62×58 mm
Capacity 174 cc
Compression ratio 7.5:1
Carburettors 1
Maximum power 11.5 @ 5 400
Fuel tank 12 l

Transmission:
Gears/Clutch 4/wmp

Electrical:
Ignition 6 v/magneto
Starting kick

Notes:

Cossack

Engine:
Type 2-str single
Bore×Stroke 52×58 mm
Capacity 123 cc
Compression ratio ...
Carburettors 1
Maximum power 9.5 @ 6 000
Fuel tank 11.3 l

Transmission:
Gears/Clutch 4/wmp

Electrical:
Ignition 6 v/magneto
Starting kick

Notes:

Planeta Sport

Braking:
Front/Rear 200 mm drums
Front tyres 3.00×19 road
Rear tyres 3.50×18 road

Suspension:
Front/Rear T/SA

Dimensions:
Ground clearance 175 mm
Seat height 790 mm
Wheelbase 1 340 mm
Overall length 1 980 mm
Dry weight 135 kg

Performance:
Top speed 140 km/h
Fuel consumption ...

Voskhod

Braking:
Front/Rear 125 mm drums
Front tyres 3.25×16 road
Rear tyres 3.25×16 road

Suspension:
Front/Rear T/SA

Dimensions:
Ground clearance 136 mm
Seat height 762 mm
Wheelbase 1 300 mm
Overall length 2 000 mm
Dry weight 112 kg

Performance:
Top speed 110 km/h
Fuel consumption 2.8 l/100 km

Minsk

Braking:
Front/Rear 125 mm drums
Front tyres 2.50×19 road
Rear tyres 2.50×19 road

Suspension:
Front/Rear T/SA

Dimensions:
Ground clearance 165 mm
Seat height 815 mm
Wheelbase 1 260 mm
Overall length 1 870 mm
Dry weight 100 kg

Performance:
Top speed 90 km/h
Fuel consumption ...

CZ (Czechoslavákia) 471

Engine:
Type 2-str single
Bore × Stroke 52 × 58 mm
Capacity 246.35 cc
Compression ratio 9.3 : 1
Carburettors 1/24 mm Jikov
Maximum power 17 @ 5 250
Fuel tank 13 l

Transmission:
Gears/Clutch 4/wmp

Electrical:
Ignition 6 v/14 Ah/b&c/D
Starting kick

Notes: Available in enduro form.

Braking:
Front/Rear 160 mm drums
Front tyres 3.00 × 18 road
Rear tyres 3.25 × 18 road

Suspension:
Front/Rear T/SA

Dimensions:
Ground clearance 120 mm
Seat height 787 mm
Wheelbase 1 330 mm
Overall length 2 020 mm
Dry weight 142 kg

Performance:
Top speed 120 km/h
Fuel consumption 4.2 l/100 km

CZ 477

Engine:
Type 2-str single
Bore × Stroke 58 × 65 mm
Capacity 171.7 cc
Compression ratio 8.6 : 1
Carburettors 1/26 mm Jikov
Maximum power 15 @ 5 600
Fuel tank 11.5 l

Transmission:
Gears/Clutch 4/wmp

Electrical:
Ignition 6 v/7½ Ah/b&c/D
Starting kick

Notes: Model 482 is Trail Special with alternative gear ratios.

Braking:
Front/Rear 160 mm drums
Front tyres 2.75 × 18 road
Rear tyres 3.00 × 18 road

Suspension:
Front/Rear T/SA

Dimensions:
Ground clearance 170 mm
Seat height 787 mm
Wheelbase 1 295 mm
Overall length 1 980 mm
Dry weight 112 kg

Performance:
Top speed 110 km/h
Fuel consumption 4 l/100 km

CZ 476

Engine:
Type 2-str single
Bore × Stroke 52 × 58 mm
Capacity 123.5 cc
Compression ratio 8.6 : 1
Carburettors 1/24 mm Jikov
Maximum power 11 @ 5 500
Fuel tank 11.5 l

Transmission:
Gears/Clutch 4/wmp

Electrical:
Ignition 6 v/7½ Ah/b&c/D
Starting kick

Notes: For complete Czechoslovak range see under Jawa, page 88.

Braking:
Front/Rear 160 mm drums
Front tyres 2.75 × 18 road
Rear tyres 3.00 × 18 road

Suspension:
Front/Rear T/SA

Dimensions:
Ground clearance 170 mm
Seat height 787 mm
Wheelbase 1 295 mm
Overall length 1 980 mm
Dry weight 111 kg

Performance:
Top speed 96 km/h
Fuel consumption 3.5 l/100 km

Demm (Italy)

Demm mopeds have been in production since the early fifties. The firm of Daldi & Matteucci was originally a manufacturer of car and truck gears but it now produces a wide range of 50 cc mopeds. The Mk III Dove is a well-established model but the range also includes single and multi-speed road and off-road machines. The company produces all its own power units and has in the past also made up to 175 cc lightweight motorcycles.

Head Office: Fratelli Daldi & Matteucci S.p.A., 20124 Milano – via Pirelli, 16/A, Italy.

UK Concessionaires: Motorised Cycles Ltd, 87 Beddington Lane, Croydon CRO 4TD.

Demm — Mk III Dove

Engine:
Type   2-str single
Bore × Stroke   38.80 × 42 mm
Capacity   49.65 cc
Compression ratio   8.5:1
Carburettors   1/12 mm Dell'Orto
Maximum power   2 @ 5600
Fuel tank   3.4 l

Transmission:
Gears/Clutch   single/A

Electrical:
Ignition   6 v/magneto
Starting   pedal

Notes:

Braking:
Front/Rear 130 mm dm/110 mm dm
Front tyres   2.25 × 16 road
Rear tyres   2.25 × 16 road

Suspension:
Front/Rear   T/SA

Dimensions:
Ground clearance   190 mm
Seat height   790 mm
Wheelbase   1140 mm
Overall length   1630 mm
Dry weight   ...

Performance:
Top speed   40 km/h
Fuel consumption   1.5 l/100 km

Derbi (Spain)

The Spanish firm of Derbi was founded by Señor Rabosa after World War II and is still a family concern. The modern Derbi factory concentrates on small bikes and since 1965 has won many speed championships in the 50 and 125 cc classes. The Angelo Nieto replica is a copy of the Francisco Tombas designed racing machine on which Nieto, the Spanish champion, won the 50 cc world championship in 1969, 1970 and 1972, and is available for purchase by the general public. The Derbi range is marketed in many European countries and the latest models are the 2002 twin, which in SL form develops 26 bhp and has a top speed of 145 km/h, and the 49 cc Cross dual-purpose machine.

Head Office: Derbi Nacional Motor, S.A., Mollet – Martorellas (Barcelona), Spain.

UK Concessionaire: Derby Concessionaires Ltd, Bremar House, 27 Sale Place, London W2 1PT.

Derbi 2002

Engine:
Type 2-str twin
Bore × Stroke 51.5 × 45 mm
Capacity 187.5 cc
Compression ratio 10 : 1
Carburettors 2/24 mm Dell'Orto
Maximum power 23 @ 7 600
Fuel tank 14 l

Transmission:
Gears/Clutch 6/wmp

Electrical:
Ignition 12 v/ℓ/magneto
Starting kick

Notes: Grand Prix SL model has electric start and optional disc brake.

Braking:
Front 170 mm dm/150 mm dm
Front tyres 2.75 × 18 road
Rear tyres 3.00 × 18 road

Suspension:
Front T/SA

Dimensions:
Ground clearance 160 mm
Seat height 790 mm
Wheelbase 1 290 mm
Overall length 2 050 mm
Dry weight 110 kg

Performance:
Top speed 135 km/h
Fuel consumption 5.7 l/100 km

Derbi

Engine:
Type 2-str single
Bore×Stroke 38×43 mm
Capacity 48.767 cc
Compression ratio ...
Carburettors 1/24 mm IRZ
Maximum power 15.5 @ 15 000
Fuel tank ...

Transmission:
Gears/Clutch 6/wmp

Electrical:
Ignition 6 v/ε
Starting kick

Notes: Angelo Nieto replica racer.

Carreras Cliente

Braking:
Front/Rear drums
Front tyres 2.00×18 road
Rear tyres 2.25×18 road

Suspension:
Front/Rear T/SA

Dimensions:
Ground clearance 200 mm
Seat height 630 mm
Wheelbase 1 226 mm
Overall length 1 760
Dry weight ...

Performance:
Top speed 165 km/h
Fuel consumption ...

Derbi

Engine:
Type 2-str single
Bore×Stroke 38×43 mm
Capacity 48.767 cc
Compression ratio 9:1
Carburettors 1/14 mm Dell'Orto
Maximum power 4.5 @ 5 700
Fuel tank 6.4 l

Transmission:
Gears/Clutch 4/wmp

Electrical:
Ignition 6 v/magneto
Starting kick

Notes: Also available in 3-speed version.

GT 4-V

Braking:
Front/Rear 105 mm drums
Front tyres 2.25×18 road
Rear tyres 2.25×18 road

Suspension:
Front/Rear T/SA

Dimensions:
Ground clearance 160 mm
Seat height 790 mm
Wheelbase 1 170 mm
Overall length 1 830 mm
Dry weight 54.5 kg

Performance:
Top speed 75 km/h
Fuel consumption 2.25 l/100 km

Derbi

Engine:
Type 2-str single
Bore×Stroke 38×43 mm
Capacity 48.767 cc
Compression ratio 9:1
Carburettors 1/14 mm Dell'Orto
Maximum power 4.5 @ 5 700
Fuel tank 3.5 l

Transmission:
Gears/Clutch 4/wmp

Electrical:
Ignition 6 v/magneto
Starting kick

Notes: Also available in road version as Correcaminos E.

Cross

Braking:
Front/Rear 105 mm drums
Front tyres 2.25×18 trials
Rear tyres 2.50×17 trials

Suspension:
Front/Rear T/SA (3-pos.)

Dimensions:
Ground clearance 280 mm
Seat height 756 mm
Wheelbase 1 180 mm
Overall length 1 770 mm
Dry weight ...

Performance:
Top speed 70 km/h
Fuel consumption 2.25 l/100 km

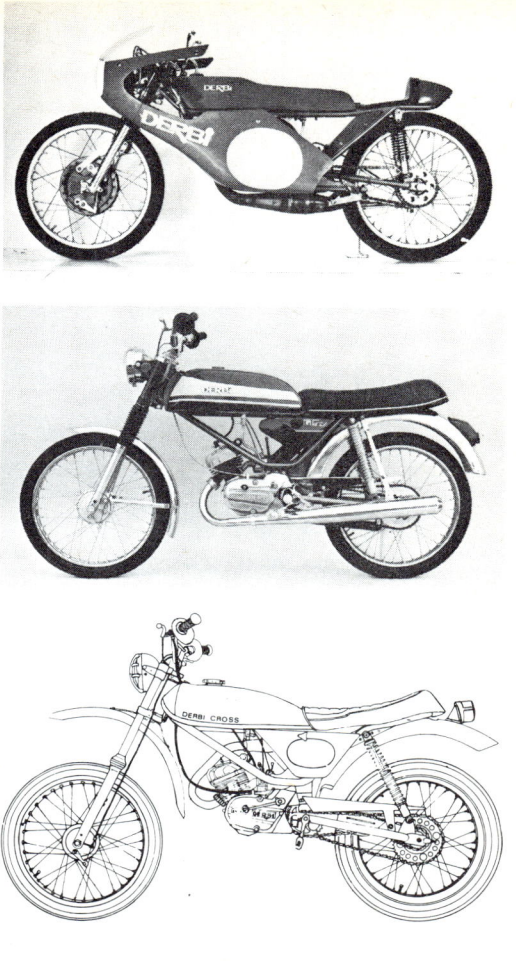

DKW (West Germany)

Wankel 2000

Engine:
Type Sachs Wankel rotary
Bore×Stroke not applicable
Capacity 2/294 cc
Compression ratio 8.5:1
Carburettors 1/32 mm Bing
Maximum power 32 @ 6 500
Fuel tank 18 l

Transmission:
Gears/Clutch 6/wmp

Electrical:
Ignition 12v/15 Ah/ε/A
Starting electric

Notes:

Braking:
Front/Rear 300 mm dc/180 mm dm
Front tyres 3.00×18 road
Rear tyres 3.25×18 road

Suspension:
Front/Rear T/SA (5-pos.)

Dimensions:
Ground clearance 160 mm
Seat height 780 mm
Wheelbase 1 330 mm
Overall length 2 050 mm
Dry weight 173 kg

Performance:
Top speed 150 km/h
Fuel consumption 6.6 l/100 km

DKW 125 GS

Engine:
Type 2-str Sachs single
Bore×Stroke 54×54 mm
Capacity 122 cc
Compression ratio 11.8:1
Carburettors 1/Bing
Maximum power 19 @ 8 800
Fuel tank 9.5 l

Transmission:
Gears/Clutch 6/wmp

Electrical:
Ignition 6 v/magneto
Starting kick

Notes: Moto-cross version available, also 50 GS model.

Braking:
Front/Rear 140 mm drums
Front tyres 3.00×21 trials
Rear tyres 4.00×18 trials

Suspension:
Front/Rear T/SA (3-pos.)

Dimensions:
Ground clearance 190 mm
Seat height 800 mm
Wheelbase 1 360 mm
Overall length 2 000 mm
Dry weight 99 kg

Performance:
Top speed 100 km/h
Fuel consumption 5 l/100 km

DKW 505p

Engine:
Type 2-str horizontal single
Bore×Stroke 38×42 mm
Capacity 49 cc
Compression ratio 8:1
Carburettors 1/10 mm Bing
Maximum power 1.8 @ 4 500
Fuel tank 4 l

Transmission:
Gears/Clutch single/A

Electrical:
Ignition 6 v/magneto
Starting pedal

Notes: Also available in 2-speed version.

Braking:
Front/Rear 90 mm drums
Front tyres 2.00×21 road
Rear tyres 2.00×21 road

Suspension:
Front/Rear T/SA

Dimensions:
Ground clearance 120 mm
Seat height 810 mm
Wheelbase 1 110 mm
Overall length 1 700 mm
Dry weight 42 kg

Performance:
Top speed 40 km/h
Fuel consumption 1.4 l/100 km

DKW
508S City bike

Engine:
Type 2-str horizontal single
Bore×Stroke 38×42 mm
Capacity 49 cc
Compression ratio 8:1
Carburettors 1/10 mm Bing
Maximum power 1.5 @ 3750
Fuel tank 2.75 l

Transmission:
Gears/Clutch single/A

Electrical:
Ignition 6 v/magneto
Starting pedal

Notes:

Braking:
Front/Rear 90 mm drums
Front tyres 2.50×9 road
Rear tyres 2.50×9 road

Suspension:
Front/Rear T/rigid

Dimensions:
Ground clearance 60 mm
Seat height 710 mm
Wheelbase 910 mm
Overall length 1 320 mm
Dry weight 42 kg

Performance:
Top speed 25 km/h
Fuel consumption 1.4 l/100 km

DKW is the export name of the Zweirad Union AG which in 1966 merged the interests of DKW, Express and Victoria with the Hercules company of Nürnberg to create the largest manufacturer of two-wheelers in Germany. The current range includes the 25 km/h Accu electric-powered moped, a number of off-road machines and 50 and 125 cc roadsters with front-disc braking.

The Hercules factory which produces DKWs was founded by Carl Marschütz, his first motorcycles appearing in 1905. Since 1954 Hercules bikes have been very successful in moto-cross and ISDT competition and currently the K125 is the motorcycle choice of the German Federal Forces. During the 1930s DKW was the largest manufacturer of motorcycles in the world and pioneered many developments in 2-stroke design. DKW was founded by a Dane, Jorgen Rasmussen, in 1907 at Zschopau (see MZ).

Head Office: Zweirad Union AG, 85 Nürnberg 1, Nopitschstrasse 70, West Germany.

UK Concessionaires: Sachs-DKW (UK) Ltd, The Scotlands Industrial Estate, London Road, Coalville, Leicestershire LE6 2JL.

Ducati (Italy)

Ducati began manufacturing in 1954 and at first concentrated on lightweight motorcycles and scooters. In 1955 their designer, Fabio Taglioni, created the first desmodromic engine which in 125 cc single form quickly brought racing success and prestige to the factory. Production engines appeared in 1969 with sleek, cafe-racer styling; the current super sports models feature desmo valve gear.

Ducati have established themselves as single and vee-twin experts and 'Dukes' race successfully in road and off-road competitions but the latest factory development has been to parallel twin models. Ducati was nationalized in 1969 and produces some 25 000 units per year, most of which go to the home market, North America, France and the UK. Mototrans of Spain produces Ducatis under licence (see page 126) and the Swiss Condor firm use Ducati-built engines in their frames (see page 16).

Head Office: Ducati Meccanica S.p.A., Casella Postale 313 – 40100 Bologna, Italy.

UK Concessionaires: Ducati Concessionaires, 21 Crawley Road, Luton, Bedfordshire.

Ducati 900SS

Engine:
Type   4-str Desmo vee-twin
Bore × Stroke   86 × 74.4 mm
Capacity   863.9 cc
Compression ratio   9.5 : 1
Carburettors   2/40 mm Dell'Orto
Maximum power   75 @ 7 500
Fuel tank   19 l

Transmission:
Gears/Clutch   5/wmp

Electrical:
Ignition   12 v/12 Ah/ε/A
Starting   electric

Notes:

Braking:
Front/Rear   280 mm dc/225 mm dc
Front tyres   3.50 × 18 racing
Rear tyres   3.50 × 18 racing

Suspension:
Front/Rear   T/SA (3-pos.)

Dimensions:
Ground clearance   160 mm
Seat height   760 mm
Wheelbase   1 500
Overall length   2 210 mm
Dry weight   192 kg

Performance:
Top speed   225 km/h
Fuel consumption   6.2 l/100 km

Ducati

860 GT

Engine:
Type 4-str sohc vee-twin
Bore × Stroke 86 × 74.4 mm
Capacity 863.9 cc
Compression ratio 9:1
Carburettors 2/32 mm Dell'Orto
Maximum power 65.6 @ 7 000
Fuel tank 18 l

Transmission:
Gears/Clutch 5/wmp

Electrical:
Ignition 12 v/32 Ah/ε/A
Starting electric †

Notes: † Electric start optional.

Braking:
Front/Rear 280 mm dc/200 mm dm
Front tyres 3.50 × 18 road
Rear tyres 4.25 × 18 road

Suspension:
Front/Rear T/SA (3-pos.)

Dimensions:
Ground clearance 180 mm
Seat height 800 mm
Wheelbase 1 520 mm
Overall length 2 200
Dry weight 212 kg

Performance:
Top speed 190 km/h
Fuel consumption 5 l/100 km

Ducati

350 GTL

Engine:
Type 4-str sohc twin
Bore × Stroke 71.8 × 43.2 mm
Capacity 349.6 cc
Compression ratio 10:1
Carburettors 2/27 mm Dell'Orto
Maximum power 29.5 @ 8 500
Fuel tank 19 l

Transmission:
Gears/Clutch 5/wmp

Electrical:
Ignition 12 v/12 Ah/ε/A
Starting electric

Notes: 500 GTL model available (see page 192).

Braking:
Front/Rear 260 mm dc/160 mm dm
Front tyres 3.00 × 19 road
Rear tyres 3.50 × 18 road

Suspension:
Front/Rear T/SA (3-pos.)

Dimensions:
Ground clearance 170 mm
Seat height 850 mm
Wheelbase 1 400 mm
Overall length 2 080 mm
Dry weight 165 kg

Performance:
Top speed 144 km/h
Fuel consumption 3.5 l/100 km

Ducati

125 Six Days

Engine:
Type 2-str single
Bore × Stroke 54 × 54 mm
Capacity 123.7 cc
Compression ratio 12.4:1
Carburettors 1/30 mm Dell'Orto
Maximum power 21.8 @ 9 000
Fuel tank 6 l

Transmission:
Gears/Clutch 6/wmp

Electrical:
Ignition 6 v/7 Ah/ε/magneto
Starting kick

Notes:

Braking:
Front/Rear 125 mm dm/140 mm dm
Front tyres 3.00 × 21 trials
Rear tyres 3.75 × 18 trials

Suspension:
Front/Rear T/SA (gas/air)

Dimensions:
Ground clearance 220 mm
Seat height 850 mm
Wheelbase 1 420 mm
Overall length 2 160 mm
Dry weight 105 kg

Performance:
Top speed 106 km/h
Fuel consumption 3.85 l/100 km

Enfield India (India)

These traditionally styled motorcycles were first developed in Redditch, England, by the Enfield Company under the names of Bullet and Ensign, and later were manufactured in India when Enfield India Ltd was formed in 1955. Two factories near Madras and Madurai in southern India now produce 25 000 machines a year for the home market and for export to African countries. Both models have won many successes in All-India road racing and they are standard issue to both the police and the armed forces.

Enfield India retains close links with Britain through Villiers Engines Ltd whose industrial and agricultural engines are also made in Madras.

Head Office: Enfield India Ltd, Post Bag No. 1053, 3B Eldams Road, Madras-600018, India.

Enfield India

Bullet 350

Engine:
Type 4-str ohv single
Bore × Stroke 70 × 90 mm
Capacity 346 cc
Compression ratio 6.5 : 1
Carburettors ...
Maximum power 18 @ 5 500
Fuel tank 15 l

Transmission:
Gears/Clutch 4/wmp

Electrical:
Ignition ...
Starting kick

Notes:

Braking:
Front/Rear drums
Front tyres 3.00 × 18 road
Rear tyres 3.00 × 18 road

Suspension:
Front/Rear T/SA

Dimensions:
Ground clearance 140 mm
Seat height ...
Wheelbase 1 380 mm
Overall length 2 110 mm
Dry weight 162 kg

Performance:
Top speed 135 km/h
Fuel consumption 3.3 l/100 km

Enfield India — Crusader

Engine:
Type 2-str Villiers single
Bore×Stroke 59×63.5 mm
Capacity 173 cc
Compression ratio 7.4 : 1
Carburettors ...
Maximum power 7.4 @ 5 000
Fuel tank 12 l

Transmission:
Gears/Clutch 4/wmp

Electrical:
Ignition ...
Starting kick

Notes:

Braking:
Front/Rear drums
Front tyres 3.00×18 road
Rear tyres 3.00×18 road

Suspension:
Front/Rear T/SA

Dimensions:
Ground clearance 130 mm
Seat height ...
Wheelbase 1 270 mm
Overall length 2 000 mm
Dry weight 115 kg

Performance:
Top speed 95 km/h
Fuel consumption 2.5 l/100 km

Royal Enfield

The Royal Enfield Bullet models were first developed in the 1930s and appeared after World War II in both 350 and 500 cc versions featuring the then novel swing-arm rear suspension. Basically the same engine was later used in the 1950s and 60s to power the 700 cc ohv Meteor twins. The Redditch-based company was originally formed to manufacture bicycles in the 1890s and during its long history it produced a wide range of motorcycles including many popular side-car models. Its last models appeared in the mid sixties and included a 246 cc 2-stroke road racer developing 34 bhp and the 736 cc Interceptor twins. Production of all Royal Enfield bikes finally ceased in 1970.

Escorts (India)

Escorts Ltd started in 1944 and is an agency manufacturer for a wide range of mechanical equipment used in agriculture, transport and health. Amongst its products are tractors, engine parts, shock absorbers, brake equipment, farming implements and X-ray machines. Motorcycles were built between 1962 and 1965 in collaboration with WFM of Poland but the current range are Indian designed and made. The factory is 30 km from Delhi and the 1 700 workforce produce over 20 000 two-wheelers a year, mostly motorcycles. Production is planned to increase to 60 000 units a year within the next five years and will include three-wheelers. Optional extras on these comprehensively equipped machines include a saree guard for the pillion passenger. The potent GTS fun bike has a top speed of over 90 km/h.

Head Office: Escorts Ltd, Motorcycle and Scooter Division, 19/6 Mathura Road, Faridabad (Haryana), India.

Escorts Rajdoot

Notes: The Rajdoot Ranger is a de luxe model with enclosed rear chain.

Engine:
Type   2-str single
Bore × Stroke   61.5 × 58 mm
Capacity   173 cc
Compression ratio   6.6 : 1
Carburettors   1/24 mm Mikuni
Maximum power   9 @ 5 000
Fuel tank   12 l

Transmission:
Gears/Clutch   3/wmp

Electrical:
Ignition   6 v/magneto
Starting   kick

Braking:
Front/Rear   160 mm drums
Front tyres   3.00 × 19 road
Rear tyres   3.00 × 19 road

Suspension:
Front/Rear   Earles/SA

Dimensions:
Ground clearance   170 mm
Seat height   760 mm
Wheelbase   1 290 mm
Overall length   2 010 mm
Dry weight   120 kg

Performance:
Top speed   80 km/h
Fuel consumption   2.25 l/100 km

Escorts

Engine:
Type 2-str single
Bore × Stroke 61.5 × 58 mm
Capacity 173 cc
Compression ratio 6.6 : 1
Carburettors 1/24 mm Mikuni
Maximum power 9 @ 5 000
Fuel tank 6.75 l

Transmission:
Gears/Clutch 3/wmp

Electrical:
Ignition 6 v/magneto
Starting kick

Notes:

Rajdoot Scooter

Braking:
Front/Rear 160 mm drums
Front tyres 3.50 × 10 road
Rear tyres 3.50 × 10 road

Suspension:
Front/Rear Earles/SA

Dimensions:
Ground clearance 145 mm
Seat height 750 mm
Wheelbase 1 325 mm
Overall length 1 950 mm
Dry weight 120 kg

Performance:
Top speed 80 km/h
Fuel consumption 2.35 l/100 km

Escorts Rajdoot
GTS 175

Fantic (Italy)

Engine:
Type 2-str single
Bore×Stroke 52×55 mm
Capacity 123.48 cc
Compression ratio 12:1
Carburettors 1/27 mm Dell'Orto
Maximum power 19 @ 8 600
Fuel tank 9.5 l

Transmission:
Gears/Clutch 5/wmp

Electrical:
Ignition 6 v/ε/A
Starting kick

Notes:

TX 150 Caballero

Braking:
Front/Rear 124 mm dm/140 mm dm
Front tyres 3.00×21 trials
Rear tyres 4.00×18 trials

Suspension:
Front/Rear T/SA

Dimensions:
Ground clearance 265 mm
Seat height 925 mm
Wheelbase 1 440 mm
Overall length 2 150 mm
Dry weight 103 kg

Performance:
Top speed 115 km/h
Fuel consumption 4.2 l/100 km

Fantic

Engine:
Type 2-str single
Bore×Stroke 38×42 mm
Capacity 49.6 cc
Compression ratio 11:1
Carburettors 1/19 mm Dell'Orto
Maximum power 6.8 @ 8 700
Fuel tank 8 l

Transmission:
Gears/Clutch 4/wmp

Electrical:
Ignition 6 v/magneto
Starting pedal

Notes: Also 6-speed version.

GT

Braking:
Front/Rear 118 mm drums
Front tyres 2.75×17 road
Rear tyres 2.75×17 road

Suspension:
Front/Rear T/SA

Dimensions:
Ground clearance 270 mm
Seat Height 770 mm
Wheelbase 1 245 mm
Overall length 1 905 mm
Dry weight 66 kg

Performance:
Top speed 75 km/h
Fuel consumption 2.8 l/100 km

Fantic

Engine:
Type 2-str single
Bore×Stroke 38.8×42 mm
Capacity 49.6 cc
Compression ratio 11:1
Carburettors 1/19 mm Dell'Orto
Maximum power 6.2 @ 9 000
Fuel tank 8 l

Transmission:
Gears/Clutch 4/wmp

Electrical:
Ignition 6 v/magneto
Starting kick

Notes: Also 6-speed version.

Caballero 50

Braking:
Front/Rear 120 mm drums
Front tyres 2.50×19 trials
Rear tyres 3.00×17 trials

Suspension:
Front/Rear T/SA

Dimensions:
Ground clearance 270 mm
Seat height 770 mm
Wheelbase 1 250 mm
Overall length 1 855 mm
Dry weight 72 kg

Performance:
Top speed 75 km/h
Fuel consumption 2.8 l/100 km

Fantic   **TX 170 Roma**

Engine:
Type 2-str horizontal single
Bore × Stroke 38.8 × 42 mm
Capacity 49.6 cc
Compression ratio 9:1
Carburettors 1/14 mm Dell'Orto
Maximum power 2 @ 7 000
Fuel tank 4 l

Transmission:
Gears/Clutch single/A

Electrical:
Ignition 6 v/ε/A
Starting pedal

Notes: Deputy is an off-road fun bike with similar specification.

Braking:
Front/Rear 90 mm drums
Front tyres 3.00 × 10 road
Rear tyres 3.00 × 10 road

Suspension:
Front/Rear T/SA

Dimensions:
Ground clearance 160 mm
Seat height 800 mm
Wheelbase 1 075 mm
Overall length 1 530 mm
Dry weight 47 kg

Performance:
Top speed 40 km/h
Fuel consumption 2.5 l/100 km

Fantic Motor was formed in 1968 and produces sporting mopeds, lightweight motorcycles and recreational two-wheelers in a modern factory in Barzago, northern Italy. The high quality specification of Fantic machines, the powerful Minarelli engines and the imaginative styling have created a very sophisticated range of on/off road bikes which also includes two 50 cc and 125 cc chopper models with high rise handlebars and 'peanut' fuel tanks.
Head Office: Fantic Motor S.p.A., 22061 Barzago (Como), via Statale 1, Italy.
UK Concessionaires: Barron Eurotrade Ltd, Fantic House, High Street, Hornchurch, RM11 1TP.

Flandria (Belgium)

Originally a small, family firm specializing in agricultural implements and bicycles, A. Claeys Flandria is now the leading motorcycle manufacturer in the Benelux countries. First serious production of motorcycles began in 1950 although designs had existed since 1933. The home plants at Zedelgen and Zwevezele near Bruges turn out some 110 000 motorcycles and mopeds a year, as well as a range of aluminium extrusive products, bicycles, lawn-mowers and gas heaters. Overseas plants are located in France, Morocco, the Netherlands and Portugal, and export sales are world-wide. A major selling point in the extensive Flandria range is the powerful, precision-built engine which is also constructed under licence at Fiquaras in Spain.

Head Office: A. Claeys-Flandria S.A., Torhoutsteenweg 118, B-8210 Zedelgem, Belgium.

UK Concessionaires: Yieldnash Ltd, Temple House, 34/36 High Street, Sevenoaks, Kent TN13 1JG.

Flandria Starline 6

Engine:
Type   2-str single
Bore × Stroke   40 × 39.7 cc
Capacity   49.7 cc
Compression ratio   11 : 1
Carburettors   1/19 mm Dell'Orto
Maximum power   8 @ 8 000*
Fuel tank   7.5 l

Transmission:
Gears/Clutch   6/wmp

Electrical:
Ignition   6 v/magneto
Starting   kick

Notes: 4-speed version available.

Braking:
Front/Rear 190 mm dc/120 mm dm
Front tyres   2.25 × 21 road
Rear tyres   2.50 × 21 road

Suspension:
Front/Rear   T/SA

Dimensions:
Ground clearance   165 mm
Seat height   712 mm
Wheelbase   1 157 mm
Overall length   1 752 mm
Dry weight   64 kg

Performance:
Top speed   96 km/h
Fuel consumption   4.6 l/100 km

Flandria

Rekord 6

Engine:
Type 2-str single
Bore×Stroke 40×39.7 mm
Capacity 49.7 cc
Compression ratio 11:1
Carburettors 1/19 mm Dell'Orto
Maximum power 8 @ 8 000
Fuel tank 7.5 l

Transmission:
Gears/Clutch 6/wmp

Electrical:
Ignition 6 v/magneto
Starting pedal

Notes: Also 4-speed version.

Braking:
Front/Rear 120 mm drums
Front tyres 2.25×21 road
Rear tyres 2.50×21 road

Suspension:
Front/Rear T/SA

Dimensions:
Ground clearance 165 mm
Seat height 712 mm
Wheelbase 1 157 mm
Overall length 1 752 mm
Dry weight 63 kg

Performance:
Top speed 96 km/h
Fuel consumption 4.6 l/100 km

Flandria

SP 947 MS

Engine:
Type 2-str single
Bore×Stroke 40×39.7 mm
Capacity 49.7 cc
Compression ratio 10:1
Carburettors 1/19 mm Dell'Orto
Maximum power 6 @ 7 800
Fuel tank 6.8 l

Transmission:
Gears/Clutch 4/wmp

Electrical:
Ignition 6 v/magneto
Starting pedal

Notes: Motorcycle version with 6-speeds also manufactured.

Braking:
Front/Rear 122 mm drums
Front tyres 2.25×17 road
Rear tyres 2.75×17 road

Suspension:
Front/Rear T/SA

Dimensions:
Ground clearance 158 mm
Seat height 709 mm
Wheelbase 1 160 mm
Overall length 1 778 mm
Dry weight 63 kg

Performance:
Top speed 85 km/h
Fuel consumption 3.8 l/100 km

Flandria

Scorpion M

Engine:
Type 2-str single
Bore×Stroke 40×39.7 mm
Capacity 49.7 cc
Compression ratio 8.5:1
Carburettors 1/19 mm Dell'Orto
Maximum power 5.2 @ 7 300
Fuel tank 6.8 l

Transmission:
Gears/Clutch 4/wmp

Electrical:
Ignition 6 v/magneto
Starting pedal

Notes: 6-speed version and competition model with 7.2 bhp engine also available.

Braking:
Front/Rear 122 mm drums
Front tyres 2.50×19 trials
Rear tyres 3.00×17 trials

Suspension:
Front/Rear T/SA

Dimensions:
Ground clearance 260 mm
Seat height 770 mm
Wheelbase 1 150 mm
Overall length 1 800 mm
Dry weight 70 kg

Performance:
Top speed 72 km/h
Fuel consumption 3.8 l/100 km

Flandria

Engine:
Type 2-str single
Bore × Stroke 40 × 39.7 mm
Capacity 49.7 cc
Compression ratio 8.5 : 1
Carburettors 1/15 mm Bing
Maximum power 4.3 @ 7 200
Fuel tank 7 l

Transmission:
Gears/Clutch 4/wmp

Electrical:
Ignition 6 v/magneto
Starting pedal

Notes: Sport version with 19 mm Dell'Orto delivers 6 bhp with 88 km/h top speed.

Flandria

Engine:
Type 2-str single
Bore × Stroke 40 × 39.7 mm
Capacity 49.7 cc
Compression ratio 8.5 : 1
Carburettors 1/15 mm Bing
Maximum power 2.2 @ 4 500
Fuel tank 7 l

Transmission:
Gears/Clutch 4/wmp

Electrical:
Ignition 6 v/magneto
Starting pedal

Notes: Also made in automatic form.

Flandria

Engine:
Type 2-str single
Bore × Stroke 40 × 39.7 mm
Capacity 49.7 cc
Compression ratio 7.5 : 1
Carburettors 1/12 mm Encarwi
Maximum power 2.7 @ 5 500
Fuel tank 4 l

Transmission:
Gears/Clutch single/A

Electrical:
Ignition 6 v/magneto
Starting pedal

Notes: Several variations of this model available.

SP 547 M

Braking:
Front/Rear 90 mm drums
Front/tyres 2.25 × 17 road
Rear tyres 2.50 × 17 road

Suspension:
Front/Rear T/SA

Dimensions:
Ground clearance 191 mm
Seat height 745 mm
Wheelbase 1 160 mm
Overall length 1 760 mm
Dry weight 58 kg

Performance:
Top speed 72 km/h
Fuel consumption 3.5 l/100 km

SP 847 M

Braking:
Front/Rear 90 mm drums
Front tyres 3.00 × 10 road
Rear tyres 3.00 × 10 road

Suspension:
Front/Rear T/SA

Dimensions:
Ground clearance 140 mm
Seat height 648 mm
Wheelbase 970 mm
Overall length 1 460 mm
Dry weight 54 kg

Performance:
Top speed 60 km/h
Fuel consumption 2.3 l/100 km

147 FA

Braking:
Front/Rear 90 mm drums
Front tyres 2.25 × 17 road
Rear tyres 2.25 × 17 road

Suspension:
Front/Rear T/SA

Dimensions:
Ground clearance 121 mm
Seat height 749-800 mm
Wheelbase 1 107 mm
Overall length 1 717 mm
Dry weight 44 kg

Performance:
Top speed 48 km/h
Fuel consumption 2.1 l/100 km

Garelli (Italy)

KL 100

Engine:
Type 2-str single
Bore × Stroke 48 × 44 mm
Capacity 80 cc
Compression ratio 11:1
Carburettors 1/19 mm Dell'Orto
Maximum power 9.5 @ 8 000
Fuel tank 11 l

Transmission:
Gears/Clutch 5/wmp

Electrical:
Ignition 6 v/ε
Starting kick

Notes: Also in cross version.

Braking:
Front/Rear 160 mm drums
Front tyres 2.50 × 19 road
Rear tyres 2.75 × 19 road

Suspension:
Front/Rear T/SA (3-pos.)

Dimensions:
Ground clearance 230 mm
Seat height 800 mm
Wheelbase 1 230 mm
Overall length 1 860 mm
Dry weight ...

Performance:
Top speed 90 km/h.
Fuel consumption ...

Garelli

Engine:
Type 2-str single
Bore × Stroke 40 × 39 mm
Capacity 49 cc
Compression ratio 12:1
Carburettors 1/20 mm Dell'Orto
Maximum power 6.2 @ 8 500
Fuel tank 9 l

Transmission:
Gears/Clutch 4/wmp

Electrical:
Ignition 6 v/magneto
Starting pedal

Notes:

Junior Rekord

Braking:
Front/Rear 120 mm drums
Front tyres 2.25 × 19 road
Rear tyres 2.50 × 19 road

Suspension:
Front/Rear T/SA

Dimensions:
Ground clearance 230 mm
Seat height 790 mm
Wheelbase 1 170 mm
Overall length 1 800 mm
Dry weight 74 kg

Performance:
Top speed 88 km/h
Fuel consumption 3.6 l/100 km

Garelli

Engine:
Type 2-str single
Bore × Stroke 40 × 39 mm
Capacity 49 cc
Compression ratio 12:1
Carburettors 1/20 mm Dell'Orto
Maximum power 6.2 @ 8 500
Fuel tank 9 l

Transmission:
Gears/Clutch 4/wmp

Electrical:
Ignition 6 v/magneto
Starting pedal

Notes:

50 cc Cross

Braking:
Front/Rear 127 mm drums
Front tyres 2.50 × 19 trials
Rear tyres 2.50 × 17 trials

Suspension:
Front/Rear T/SA

Dimensions:
Ground clearance 230 mm
Seat height 790 mm
Wheelbase 1 170 mm
Overall length 1 800 mm
Dry weight 74 kg

Performance:
Top speed 80 km/h
Fuel consumption 3.6 l/100 km

Garelli   **Bimatic**

Engine:
Type 2-str single
Bore/Stroke 40 × 39 mm
Capacity 49 cc
Compression ratio 7 : 1
Carburettors 1/14 mm Dell'Orto
Maximum power 1.4 @ 5 000
Fuel tank 4.5 l

Transmission:
Gears/Clutch 2/A

Electrical:
Ignition 6 v/magneto
Starting pedal

Notes: Also 3-speed Concorde and automatic Gulp and Concorde Matic models.

Braking:
Front/Rear 114 mm drums
Front tyres 2.25 × 16 road
Rear tyres 2.25 × 16 road

Suspension:
Front/Rear T/SA

Dimensions:
Ground clearance 120 mm
Seat height 750 mm
Wheelbase 1 090 mm
Overall length 1 620 mm
Dry weight 57 kg

Performance:
Top speed 53 km/h
Fuel consumption 2.7 l/100 km

Garelli was established in 1913 and in the early twenties produced 350 cc 2-stroke singles which were very successful in racing. After the war it produced the Mosquito engines for bicycles and in 1967 merged with the Agrati organization. The factory at Sesto San Giovanni now concentrates on the manufacture of 2-stroke engines. A. Agrati & Figli S.p.A. dates from 1900 and its Monticello factory assembles Garelli mopeds and light motorcycles. The wide range of moped models includes mini bikes and the Katia moped which is also made in electric-powered form with a speed of 30 km/h and a range of 50 km. The company also makes components for bicycles and motorcycles.

Head Office: Agrati-Garelli G.I., S.p.A., 22068 Monticello Brianza(CO), Italy.
UK Concessionaires: Agrati Sales (UK) Ltd, St Mark's Street, Nottingham, NG3 1DA.

Gilera (Italy)

Gilera was formed in 1909 and soon established itself as a producer of powerful 500 cc engines. During the thirties water-cooled Gilera Fours won great prestige for the factory and in 1937 held the world speed record at 274 km/h. During the 1950s Gilera Fours proved unbeatable but in 1957 the company announced its retirement from road racing. The sports interests of the present company are now devoted to trial and cross competitions.

At the end of 1969, financial difficulties nearly ended the Gilera line but its assets and name were acquired by Piaggio, makers of Vespa scooters. The current range includes sport, touring and off-road mopeds and single-cylinder lightweights such as the 125 and 150 cc Arcore models.

Head Office: Gilera, 20043 Arcore (MI), via Cesare Battisti 68, Italy.
UK Concessionaires: Douglas Ltd, 2, Oak Lane, Fishponds, Bristol, BS5 7XB.

Gilera

Engine:
Type 2-str single
Bore × Stroke 38.4 × 43 mm
Capacity 49.8 cc
Compression ratio 12:1
Carburettors 1/18 mm Dell'Orto
Maximum power 6.2 @ 7 000*
Fuel tank 6.8 l

Transmission:
Gears/Clutch 5/wmp

Electrical:
Ignition 6 v/magneto
Starting kick

Notes: Also 4-speed moped version and 5-speed Trial R.S.

Touring RS

Braking:
Front/Rear 102 mm drums
Front tyres 2.50 × 17 road
Rear tyres 2.75 × 17 road

Suspension:
Front/Rear T/SA

Dimensions:
Ground clearance 180 mm
Seat height 800 mm
Wheelbase 1 160 mm
Overall length 1 780 mm
Dry weight 68 kg

Performance:
Top speed 85 km/h
Fuel consumption ...

Gilera
Enduro Moped

Engine:
Type 2-str single
Bore × Stroke 38.4 × 43 mm
Capacity 49.8 cc
Compression ratio 12:1
Carburettors 1/18 mm Dell'Orto
Maximum power 4.2 @ 5 500
Fuel tank 6.8 l

Transmission:
Gears/Clutch 4/wmp

Electrical:
Ignition 6 v/magneto
Starting pedal

Notes: 4-speed trial moped also available.

Braking:
Front/Rear 102 mm drums
Front tyres 2.50 × 19 trials
Rear tyres 3.00 × 17 trials

Suspension:
Front/Rear T/SA

Dimensions:
Ground clearance 220 mm
Seat height 800 mm
Wheelbase 1 190 mm
Overall length 1 880 mm
Dry weight 73 kg

Performance:
Top speed 64 km/h
Fuel consumption ...

Gilera
4-speed Trial Moped

Harley-Davidson (USA)

The Harley-Davidson Company was incorporated in 1907 although the first Harley bike, a 3 hp belt-driven machine with a DeDion engine had been constructed by William Harley and his friends the Davidson brothers in 1902. In Europe the World War I effort resulted in motorcycle production ceasing in Britain and countries all over the world turned to the American manufacturers for the motorcycles they needed and this gave a big boost to Harley-Davidson production. By 1917 18 000 bikes were leaving the Milwaukee factory each year, many destined for despatch duties with the American forces now in Europe. During the twenties and thirties Harley-Davidson established its brand image with huge, long-stroke vee-twins like the WL 1 100 cc side-valve which became the US Army's first choice in World War II. Mechanical innovations then included interchangeable wheels, four-cam valve operation, high-compression aluminium pistons and the famous balloon tyres. The post-war 1 100 ohv twin featured hydraulic valve lifters and aluminium heads previously used only on aircraft engines.

Harley Davidson   FLX 1200 Electra Glide

Engine:
Type 4-str ohv vee-twin
Bore×Stroke 87.3×100.8 mm
Capacity 1 207 cc
Compression ratio 8:1
Carburettors 1/38 mm Tillotson
Maximum power 66 @ 5 200 (p)
Fuel tank 18 l

Transmission:
Gears/Clutch 4/dmp

Electrical:
Ignition 12 v/32 Ah/b&c/A
Starting electric

Notes: Also FX 1 200 Super Glide with or without electric start.

Braking:
Front/Rear 254 mm discs
Front tyres 5.10×16 road
Rear tyres 5.10×16 road

Suspension:
Front/Rear T/SA (3-pos.)

Dimensions:
Ground clearance 152 mm
Seat height 838 mm
Wheelbase 1 572 mm
Overall length 2 261 mm
Dry weight 317 kg

Performance:
Top speed 170 km/h
Fuel consumption 6 l/100 km (p)

Harley Davidson   XL 1000

Engine:
Type 4-str ohc vee-twin
Bore×Stroke 80.9×96.8 mm
Capacity 997.5 cc
Compression ratio 9:1
Carburettors 1/38 mm Tillotson
Maximum power 61 @ 6 200 (p)
Fuel tank 10 l

Transmission:
Gears/Clutch 4/wmp

Electrical:
Ignition 12 v/7 Ah/b&c/D
Starting electric

Notes: XLCH has kick start.

Braking:
Front/Rear 254 mm dc/203 mm dm
Front tyres 3.75×19 road
Rear tyres 4.25×18 road

Suspension:
Front/Rear T/SA (3-pos.)

Dimensions:
Ground clearance 165 mm
Seat height 749 mm
Wheelbase 1 485 mm
Overall length 2 216 mm
Dry weight 238 kg

Performance:
Top speed 193 km/h
Fuel consumption …

Harley Davidson   SS 250

Engine:
Type 2-str single
Bore×Stroke 72×59.6 mm
Capacity 242.6 cc
Compression ratio 10.3:1
Carburettors 1/32 mm Dell'Orto
Maximum power …
Fuel tank 11 l

Transmission:
Gears/Clutch 5/wmp

Electrical:
Ignition 12 v/ε/A
Starting kick

Notes: SS 175 also available.

Braking:
Front/Rear 135 mm drums
Front tyres 3.00×21 road
Rear tyres 4.00×18 road

Suspension:
Front/Rear T/SA (3-pos.)

Dimensions:
Ground clearance 228 mm
Seat height 812 mm
Wheelbase 1 372 mm
Overall length 2 146 mm
Dry weight 136 kg

Performance:
Top speed 136 km/h
Fuel consumption 4.2 l/100 km (p)

Harley Davidson   SX 175

Engine:
Type 2-str single
Bore×Stroke 61×59.6 mm
Capacity 174.1 cc
Compression ratio 10.7:1
Carburettors 1/27 mm Dell'Orto
Maximum power …
Fuel tank 11 l

Transmission:
Gears/Clutch 5/wmp

Electrical:
Ignition 12 v/ε/A
Starting kick

Notes: Also SX 250 and SXT 125 models.

Braking:
Front/Rear 135 mm drums
Front tyres 3.00×19 trials
Rear tyres 3.50×18 trials

Suspension:
Front/Rear T/SA (5-pos.)

Dimensions:
Ground clearance 190 mm
Seat height 800 mm
Wheelbase 1 372 mm
Overall length 2 146 mm
Dry weight 127 kg

Performance:
Top speed 120 km/h
Fuel consumption …

Harley Davidson   SS 125

Engine:
Type   2-str single
Bore × Stroke   57 × 50 mm
Capacity   123.15 cc
Compression ratio   10.8:1
Carburettors   1/27 mm Dell'Orto
Maximum power   ...
Fuel tank   10.2 l

Transmission:
Gears/Clutch   5/wmp

Electrical:
Ignition   12 v/b&c/A
Starting   kick

Notes:

Braking:
Front/Rear   135 mm drums
Front tyres   3.00 × 19 road
Rear tyres   3.50 × 18 road

Suspension:
Front/Rear   T/SA (3-pos.)

Dimensions:
Ground clearance   185 mm
Seat height   812 mm
Wheelbase   1 360 mm
Overall length   2 143 mm
Dry weight   109 kg

Performance:
Top speed   105 km/h
Fuel consumption   ...

In 1947 the first Harley 2-stroke appeared, and a variety of lightweights were added to the range following the formation of Aermacchi Harley-Davidson S.p.A. in Varese, Italy, in 1960. Harleys have always been identified with police work and since 1907 they have been adopted by police forces all round the world. In sports competition they live up to their reputation as Number 1 particularly in North America where they have dominated the national championships. In 1974 and 1975 Harley won the 250 cc world championship with the RR250 bike.

In 1967 Harley was taken over by the American Machine and Foundry Company whose international headquarters are now in Geneva. The recreational vehicle division manufactures golf cars, lawn-mowers, bicycles and the big Harley roadsters in USA, and a wide range of road and trial bikes from 90 to 350 cc in Italy.

Head Office: Harley-Davidson Motor Co., Inc., 3700 West Juneau Avenue, Milwaukee, Wisconsin 53201, USA.
UK Concessionaires: AMF International Ltd, 25–8 Old Burlington Street, London W1X 2BA.

Honda (Japan)

Honda, the world's biggest motorcycle manufacturer, began in 1948 when Soichiro Honda first began using surplus army engines to power bicycles. The first Honda-designed engine was a 50 cc 2-stroke and by 1949 the small Hamamatsu factory had already progressed to producing engines and frames for the Dream D model. During the 1950s the switch was made to 4-stroke engines and 1958 witnessed the introduction of the 50 cc C-100 with step-thru frame which was to become Honda's most popular model, creating an entirely new world market for two-wheelers.

In 1959 the American Honda company was established, forecasting Honda's huge penetration into the US market, and the involvement with motorcycle racing began which was to bring enormous prestige and developmental benefits. Honda's peak in racing was achieved in 1966 when it won all five solo world championships. Within the short space of twenty years Honda motorcycle production had reached 10 million units with a range extending from the little P50 moped to the CB450, but also including the manufacture of cars, trucks, power implements for farming, boat engines and portable generators. In 1969 the first of the superbikes was launched with the 750 Four, and this led to multi-cylinder 500s and 350s. Since then the number of models has risen to over thirty and development has been concentrated on refinements such as electric start and disc braking, a huge range of 2- and 4-stroke enduro machines especially for the US market and the massive, shaft-driven 1 000 cc Gold Wing which appeared in 1974 as one of a new breed of 'hyper-bikes'. In fifteen years annual production had risen from just over 250 000 to more than 2 000 000.

Honda engines are built to extremely precise tolerances, and the highly automated factories at Hamamatsu and Suzuka produce around two million units each year, of which some 70 per cent is exported. Honda has brought motorcycles to a high degree of technical sophistication, comfort and reliability; typical of its technical achievement was the first mass-production of an efficient 50 cc 4-stroke engine with overhead camshaft. Honda bikes are assembled in 30 overseas factories in 25 different countries and plans exist to assemble trucks and motorcycles in the Middle East. Almost half the total Japanese exports of motorcycles are Honda and their annual output exceeds the total national production of France, Austria, West Germany and Britain together. Indeed, in much of the world today the name Honda has become synonymous with motorcycles whether for work or leisure.

Head Office: Honda Motor Co. Ltd, 27–8, 6-chome, Jingu-mae, Shibuya-ku, Tokyo, Japan.
Main Factory: Suzuka Works, 1907, Hirata-cho, Suzuka-shi, Mie-ken, Japan.
UK Concessionaires: Honda (UK) Ltd, Power Road, Chiswick, London W4 5YT.

Honda

Engine:
Type 4-str ohc flat four
Bore × Stroke 72 × 51.4 mm
Capacity 999 cc
Compression ratio 9.2:1
Carburettors 4/32 mm Keihin
Maximum power 80 @ 7000
Fuel tank 19 l

Transmission:
Gears/Clutch 5/wmp

Electrical:
Ignition 12 v/20 Ah/b&c/A
Starting electric

Notes: Water cooled, shaft drive.

GL 1000 Gold Wing

Braking:
Front/Rear 267 mm dc/292 mm dc
Front tyres 3.50 × 19 road
Rear tyres 4.50 × 17 road

Suspension:
Front/Rear T/SA (5-pos.)

Dimensions:
Ground clearance 150 mm
Seat height 799 mm
Wheelbase 1 545 mm
Overall length 2 305 mm
Dry weight 259 kg

Performance:
Top speed 210 km/h (p)
Fuel consumption 7.2 l/100 km (p)

Honda

Engine:
Type 4-str ohc four
Bore × Stroke 61 × 63 mm
Capacity 736 cc
Compression ratio 9.2:1
Carburettors 4/28 mm Keihin
Maximum power 67 @ 8000
Fuel tank 17 l

Transmission:
Gears/Clutch 5/wmp

Electrical:
Ignition 12 v/14 Ah/b&c/A
Starting electric

Notes:

CB 750F

Braking:
Front/Rear 300 mm dc/178 mm dm
Front tyres 3.25 × 19 road
Rear tyres 4.00 × 18 road

Suspension:
Front/Rear T/SA (5-pos.)

Dimensions:
Ground clearance 140 mm
Seat height 810 mm
Wheelbase 1 470 mm
Overall length 2 160 mm
Dry weight 241 kg

Performance:
Top speed 185 km/h (p)
Fuel consumption 6 l/100 km (p)

Honda

Engine:
Type 4-str dohc twin
Bore × Stroke 70 × 64.8 mm
Capacity 498 cc
Compression ratio 8.5:1
Carburettors 2/32 mm Keihin
Maximum power 42 @ 8000
Fuel tank 16 l

Transmission:
Gears/Clutch 5/wmp

Electrical:
Ignition 12 v/12 Ah/b&c/A
Starting electric

Notes: Also CB 500 four model, and in USA CB 550 four.

CB 500T

Braking:
Front/Rear 230 mm dc/180 mm dm
Front tyres 3.25 × 19 road
Rear tyres 3.75 × 18 road

Suspension:
Front/Rear T/SA (5-pos.)

Dimensions:
Ground clearance 140 mm
Seat height 810 mm
Wheelbase 1 410 mm
Overall length 2 140 mm
Dry weight 193 kg

Performance:
Top speed 163 km/h (p)
Fuel consumption 5.5 l/100 km (p)

Honda
CB 400F

Engine:
Type 4-str ohc four
Bore × Stroke 51.0 × 50 mm
Capacity 408 cc
Compression ratio 9.4:1
Carburettors 2/20 mm Keihin
Maximum power 37 @ 8 500
Fuel tank 14 l

Transmission:
Gears/Clutch 6/wmp

Electrical:
Ignition 12 v/12 Ah/b&c/A
Starting electric

Notes:

Braking:
Front/Rear 214 mm dc/160 mm dm
Front tyres 3.00 × 18 road
Rear tyres 3.50 × 18 road

Suspension:
Front/Rear T/SA (5-pos.)

Dimensions:
Ground clearance 150 mm
Seat height 790 mm
Wheelbase 1 355 mm
Overall length 2 040 mm
Dry weight 170 kg

Performance:
Top speed 165 km/h (p)
Fuel consumption 5 l/100 km (p)

Honda
CB 200

Engine:
Type 4-str ohc twin
Bore × Stroke 55.5 × 41 mm
Capacity 198 cc
Compression ratio 9:1
Carburettors 2/20 mm Keihin
Maximum power 17 @ 9 000
Fuel tank 9 l

Transmission:
Gears/Clutch 5/wmp

Electrical:
Ignition 12 v/9 Ah/b&c/A
Starting electric

Notes: Also available as CB 250 and CB 360.

Braking:
Front/Rear 240 mm dc/150 mm dm
Front tyres 2.75 × 18 road
Rear tyres 3.00 × 18 road

Suspension:
Front/Rear T/SA

Dimensions:
Ground clearance 155 mm
Seat height 780 mm
Wheelbase 1 290 mm
Overall length 1 935 mm
Dry weight 132 kg

Performance:
Top speed 125 km/h (p)
Fuel consumption 4.5 l/100 km (p)

Honda
XL 250

Engine:
Type 4-str ohc single
Bore × Stroke 74 × 57.8 mm
Capacity 248 cc
Compression ratio 9.1:1
Carburettors 1/28 mm Keihin
Maximum power 20 @ 8 000*
Fuel tank 8 l

Transmission:
Gears/Clutch 5/wmp

Electrical:
Ignition 6 v/6 Ah/magneto
Starting kick

Notes: MT 250 Elsinore 2-str trial bike and whole range of XL 100, 125, 175, 350 available in USA.

Braking:
Front/Rear 150 mm drums
Front tyres 2.75 × 21 trials
Rear tyres 4.00 × 18 trials

Suspension:
Front/Rear T/SA

Dimensions:
Ground clearance 190 mm
Seat height 820 mm
Wheelbase 1 385 mm
Overall length 2 120 mm
Dry weight 126 kg

Performance:
Top speed 128 km/h (p)
Fuel consumption ...

Honda   CD 175

Engine:
Type   4-str ohc twin
Bore × Stroke   52 × 41 mm
Capacity   174 cc
Compression ratio   9:1
Carburettors   1/22 mm Keihin
Maximum power   17 @ 9 000
Fuel tank   10 l

Transmission:
Gears/Clutch   4/wmp

Electrical:
Ignition   6 v/12 Ah/b&c/A
Starting   kick

Notes:

Braking:
Front/Rear   150 mm drums
Front tyres   3.00 × 17 road
Rear tyres   3.00 × 17 road

Suspension:
Front/Rear   T/SA

Dimensions:
Ground clearance   130 mm
Seat height   760 mm
Wheelbase   1 270 mm
Overall length   1 970 mm
Dry weight   132 kg

Performance:
Top speed   120 km/h (p)
Fuel consumption   ...

Honda   CB 125J

Engine:
Type   4-str ohc single
Bore × Stroke   56 × 49.5 mm
Capacity   122 cc
Compression   9.5:1
Carburettors   1/22 mm Keihin
Maximum power   14 @ 9 000
Fuel tank   7.5 l

Transmission:
Gears/Clutch   5/wmp

Electrical:
Ignition   6 v/6 Ah/b&c/A
Starting   kick

Notes: SL 125 trial version also available.

Braking:
Front/Rear   240 mm dc/110 mm dm
Front tyres   2.75 × 18 road
Rear tyres   3.00 × 17 road

Suspension:
Front/Rear   T/SA

Dimensions:
Ground clearance   160 mm
Seat height   765 mm
Wheelbase   1 205 mm
Overall length   1 880 mm
Dry weight   91 kg

Performance:
Top speed   112 km/h (p)
Fuel consumption   3 l/100 km (p)

Honda   C90

Engine:
Type   4-str ohc single
Bore × Stroke   50 × 45.6 mm
Capacity   89.5 cc
Compression ratio   8.2:1
Carburettors   1 Keihin
Maximum power   7.5 @ 9 500
Fuel tank   5.5 l

Transmission:
Gears/Clutch   3/A

Electrical:
Ignition   6 v/6 Ah/b&c/D
Starting   kick

Notes: Also available with 49 and 72 cc engines.

Braking:
Front/Rear   110 mm drums
Front tyres   2.50 × 17 road
Rear tyres   2.50 × 17 road

Suspension:
Front/Rear   LL/SA

Dimensions:
Ground clearance   130 mm
Seat height   760 mm
Wheelbase   1 190 mm
Overall length   1 830 mm
Dry weight   74 kg

Performance:
Top speed   80 km/h (p)
Fuel consumption   ...

Honda

CF 70 Chaly

Engine:
Type 4-str ohc single
Bore × Stroke 47 × 41.4 mm
Capacity 72 cc
Compression ratio 8.8:1
Carburettors 1/11 mm Keihin
Maximum power 4.5 @ 7 000
Fuel tank 2.8 l

Transmission:
Gears/Clutch 3/A

Electrical:
Ignition 6 v/4 Ah/magneto
Starting kick

Notes: Also ST 70 fun-bike model.

Braking:
Front/Rear 110 mm drums
Front tyres 3.50 × 10 road
Rear tyres 3.50 × 10 road

Suspension:
Front/Rear T/SA

Dimensions:
Ground clearance 125 mm
Seat height 700 mm
Wheelbase 1 100 km
Overall length 1 615 mm
Dry weight 70 kg

Performance:
Top speed 72 km/h (p)
Fuel consumption ...

Honda

SS 50Z

Engine:
Type 4-str ohc single
Bore × Stroke 39 × 41.4 mm
Capacity 49 cc
Compression ratio 8.8:1
Carburettors 1/12 mm Keihin
Maximum power 2.5 @ 8 000
Fuel tank 7 l

Transmission:
Gears/Clutch 4/wsp

Electrical:
Ignition 6 v/4 Ah/magneto
Starting kick

Notes:

Braking:
Front/Rear 110 mm drums
Front tyres 2.50 × 17 road
Rear tyres 2.50 × 17 road

Suspension:
Front/Rear T/SA

Dimensions:
Ground clearance 140 mm
Seat height 750 mm
Wheelbase 1 180 mm
Overall length 1 845 mm
Dry weight 73 kg

Performance:
Top speed 64 km/h (p)
Fuel consumption 2 l/100 km (p)

Honda

PC 50

Engine:
Type 4-str ohv horizontal single
Bore × Stroke 42 × 35.6 mm
Capacity 49 cc
Compression ratio 8.5:1
Carburettors 1/12 mm Keihin
Maximum power 1.8 @ 3 500
Fuel tank 3 l

Transmission:
Gears/Clutch single/A

Electrical:
Ignition 6 v/magneto
Starting pedal

Notes: Also available as PF 50MR2 and PF 50DXR.

Braking:
Front/Rear 90 mm drums
Front tyres 2.00 × 19 road
Rear tyres 2.25 × 19 road

Suspension:
Front/Rear LL/SA

Dimensions:
Ground clearance 140 mm
Seat height 780 mm
Wheelbase 1 130 mm
Overall length 1 755 mm
Dry weight 45 kg

Performance:
Top speed 50 km/h (p)
Fuel consumption 1.5 l/100 km (p)

Indian (USA)

Indian

The legend of Indian motorcycles began in 1901 when George M. Hendee, a Massachusetts bicycle manufacturer, joined forces with Oscar Hedstrom to build motorcycles. The early, red-painted singles pioneered many technical innovations such as electric starting, twist grip controls and electric lighting. Later, Indian developed its famous Scout and Big Chief vee-twins which were widely used by the police and armed forces.

In 1959 the manufacture of American Indians ceased although for a while the British firm of Brockhouse Engineering sold Royal Enfield machines with Indian tank transfers, and in the late sixties Floyd Clymer, an Indian dealer in the USA, revived the brand. The present Indian company dates from 1969 and its range of mini and lightweight enduros and trial bikes are designed in America and built in Taiwan.

Head Office: The Indian Motorcycle Company, 110 N. Doheny Drive, Beverly Hills, California 90211, USA.
UK Concessionaires: K. I. Andrews Ltd, 5 Tunnel Avenue, Greenwich, London SE10 0SA.

Indian MI 175

Engine:
Type 2-str single
Bore × Stroke 66 × 50 mm
Capacity 171 cc
Compression ratio 9:1
Carburettors 1/26 mm Mikuni
Maximum power 17 @ 7 000
Fuel tank 6 l

Transmission:
Gears/Clutch 5/wmp

Electrical:
Ignition 6 v/magneto
Starting kick

Notes:

Braking:
Front/Rear 150 mm drums
Front tyres 3.00 × 19 trials
Rear tyres 3.50 × 17 trials

Suspension:
Front/Rear T/SA

Dimensions:
Ground clearance 228 mm
Seat height 762 mm
Wheelbase 1 270 mm
Overall length ...
Dry weight 95 kg

Performance:
Top speed 112 km/h
Fuel consumption ...

Indian ME 125

Engine:
Type 2-str single
Bore×Stroke 55×52 mm
Capacity 123.48 cc
Compression ratio 9.3:1
Carburettors 1/25 mm Dell'Orto
Maximum power 16 @ 7 200
Fuel tank 6 l

Transmission:
Gears/Clutch 5/wmp

Electrical:
Ignition 6 v/magneto
Starting kick

Notes: ME 100 has 97 cc engine developing 10 bhp.

Braking:
Front/Rear 150 mm drums
Front tyres 3.00×19 trials
Rear tyres 3.50×17 trials

Suspension:
Front/Rear T/SA

Dimensions:
Ground clearance 228 mm
Seat height 762 mm
Wheelbase 1 270 mm
Overall length ...
Dry weight 81 kg

Performance:
Top speed 104 km/h
Fuel consumption ...

Indian ME 100 Enduro

Jawa/CZ (Czechoslovakia)

Jawa bikes have been in production since 1929 when Frantisek Janecek, a Czech armaments manufacturer, began building German Wanderer machines under licence. During the 1930s Jawa used Villiers engines but soon developed 2-stroke machines which were technically advanced for their time. Since the war the nationalized Jawa factory has concentrated on economy machines and their sporting reputation is based on rugged ISDT type trials and speedway rather than road racing. The CZ factory at Strakonice has concentrated on 2-strokes since 1932 although in 1955 it began producing fast 125, 250 and 350 dohc racing bikes. The reliability of CZ machines have led to them winning many world moto-cross events. The large CZ factory produces some 30 000 bikes each year and makes the engines for Jawa models.
Main factories: *Jawa*: JAWA, n.p., Tynec n. Sazavou, Czechoslovakia. *CZ*: CZM 38615 Strakonice, Czechoslovakia.
UK Concessionaires: Skoda (GB) Ltd, Motor Cycle Operations, Bergen Way, King's Lynn, Norfolk PE30 1BR.

Jawa 634/6

Engine:
Type 2-str twin
Bore × Stroke 58 × 65 mm
Capacity 343.37 cc
Compression ratio 9.2:1
Carburettors 1/26 mm Jikov
Maximum power 28 @ 5 250
Fuel tank 16 l

Transmission:
Gears/Clutch 4/wmp

Electrical:
Ignition 6 v/14 Ah/b&c/D
Starting kick

Notes: Separate oiling system.

Braking:
Front/Rear 160 mm drums
Front tyres 3.25 × 18 road
Rear tyres 3.50 × 18 road

Suspension:
Front/rear T/SA

Dimensions:
Ground clearance 203 mm
Seat height 812 mm
Wheelbase 1 350 mm
Overall length 2 080 mm
Dry weight 155 kg

Performance:
Top speed 135 km/h
Fuel consumption 4.6 l/100 km

Kawasaki (Japan)

Kawasaki is the youngest of the 'big four' Japanese motorcycle manufacturers although its origins date back to 1878 when Shozo Kawasaki started a dockyard in Tokyo. Now Kawasaki Heavy Industries Ltd is one of the world's largest group of companies making a wide range of automated industrial machinery and transportation equipment from helicopters and ships to mini motorcycles. Kawasaki began making motorcycles in 1968 with small 2-stroke scooters but since then its reputation has been built on high performance bikes with startling acceleration and performance.

Kawasaki motorcycles are exported to ninety different countries from the Akashi works near Kobe where 1 700 employees produce over 250 000 bikes annually. The plant was originally built in 1930 for the production of aeroplane parts but the present industrial complex uses the latest mass-production technology to maintain very high output rates. Overseas assembly plants are planned for Columbia, Indonesia, Nigeria, the Philippines and Taiwan, and American-built 'Kwackers' are already in production. In line with its high-performance image Kawasaki takes an active part in motorcycle racing and works riders have won many successes in recent years on 'Green Meanies'. The current range closely reflects the demands of the North American market and the road models are supported by a big selection of motocross and enduro machines. Top of the range, the Z 900, has quickly established a world-wide reputation as superbike of the year. Technically Kawasaki bikes are highly sophisticated machinery and the company has helped to pioneer innovations such as electronic ignition and full instrumentation on motorcycles. Kawasaki engineers have also paid close attention to achieving smooth, vibration-free running, efficient silencing and pollution-free exhaust emission.

Head Office: Kawasaki Heavy Industries, Nissei Kawasaki Bldg., 16–1, Nakamachi-dori, 2-chome, Ikuta-ku, Kobe-shi, Hyogo-ken, Japan.

UK Concessionaires: Kawasaki Motors (UK) Ltd, Radix House, Central Trading Estate, Staines, Middlesex TW18 4XA.

Kawasaki Z 900

Engine:
Type 4-str dohc four
Bore×Stroke 66×66 mm
Capacity 903 cc
Compression ratio 8.5:1
Carburettors 4/26 mm Mikuni
Maximum power 82 @ 8 500
Fuel tank 17 l

Transmission:
Gears/Clutch 5/wmp

Electrical:
Ignition 12 v/10 Ah/b&c/A
Starting electric

Notes:

Braking:
Front/Rear 245 mm dc/200 mm dm
Front tyres 3.25×19 road
Rear tyres 4.00×18 road

Suspension:
Front/Rear T/SA (5-pos.)

Dimensions:
Ground clearance 165 mm
Seat height 800 mm
Wheelbase 1 505 mm
Overall length 2 245 mm
Dry weight 241 kg

Performance:
Top speed 212 km/h (p)
Fuel consumption 4.2 l/100 km (p)

Kawasaki Z 750

Engine:
Type 4-str dohc twin
Bore×Stroke 78×78 mm
Capacity 745 cc
Compression ratio 8.5:1
Carburettors 2/38 mm Mikuni
Maximum power ...
Fuel tank 14.5 l

Transmission:
Gears/Clutch 5/wmp

Electrical:
Ignition 12v/12 Ah/b&c/A
Starting electric

Notes:

Braking:
Front/Rear 245 mm dc/230 mm dc
Front tyres 3.25×19 road
Rear tyres 4.00×18 road

Suspension:
Front/Rear T/SA (5-pos.)

Dimensions:
Ground clearance 155 mm
Seat height 800 mm
Wheelbase 1 450 mm
Overall length 2 180 mm
Dry weight 218 kg

Performance:
Top speed ...
Fuel consumption ...

Kawasaki KH 500

Engine:
Type 2-str triple
Bore×Stroke 60×58.8 mm
Capacity 498 cc
Compression ratio 6.8:1
Carburettors 3/28 mm Mikuni
Maximum power 59 @ 8 000
Fuel tank 16 l

Transmission:
Gears/Clutch 5/wmp

Electrical:
Ignition 12 v/9 Ah/ε/A
Starting electric

Notes:

Braking:
Front/Rear 245 mm dc/180 mm dm
Front tyres 3.25×19 road
Rear tyres 4.00×18 road

Suspension:
Front/Rear T/SA (3-pos.)

Dimensions:
Ground clearancce 145 mm
Seat height 812 mm
Wheelbase 1 410 mm
Overall length 2 125 mm
Dry weight 194 kg

Performance:
Top speed 200 km/h (p)
Fuel consumption ...

Kawasaki Z 400

Engine:
Type 4-str sohc twin
Bore × Stroke 64 × 62 mm
Capacity 398 cc
Compression ratio 9.4:1
Carburettors 2/36 mm Keihin
Maximum power 33 @ 9 000
Fuel tank 14 l

Transmission:
Gears/Clutch 5/wmp

Electrical:
Ignition 12 v/12 Ah/b&c/A
Starting electric

Notes: KH 400 is 2-stroke triple developing 42 bhp.

Braking:
Front/Rear 226 mm dc/180 mm dm
Front tyres 3.25 × 18 road
Rear tyres 3.50 × 18 road

Suspension:
Front/Rear T/SA (3-pos.)

Dimensions:
Ground clearance 125 mm
Seat height 812 mm
Wheelbase 1 370 mm
Overall length 2 080 mm
Dry weight 175 kg

Performance:
Top speed 160 km/h (p)
Fuel consumption 4.4 l/100 km (p)

Kawasaki KH250

Engine:
Type 2-str triple
Bore × Stroke 45 × 52.3 mm
Capacity 249 cc
Compression ratio 7.5:1
Carburettors 3/22 mm Mikuni
Maximum power 28 @ 7 500
Fuel tank 14 l

Transmission:
Gears/Clutch 5/wmp

Electrical:
Ignition 12 v/5.5 Ah/b&c/A
Starting kick

Notes:

Braking:
Front/Rear 226 mm dc/180 mm dm
Front tyres 3.25 × 18 road
Rear tyres 3.50 × 18 road

Suspension:
Front/Rear T/SA (3-pos.)

Dimensions:
Ground clearance 155 mm
Seat height 781 mm
Wheelbase 1 375 mm
Overall length 2 055 mm
Dry weight 154 kg

Performance:
Top speed 144 km/h (p)
Fuel consumption 6.4 l/100 km (p)

Kawasaki KE 125

Engine:
Type 2-str rotary valve single
Bore × Stroke 56 × 50.6 mm
Capacity 124 cc
Compression ratio 6.5:1
Carburettors 1/24 mm Mikuni
Maximum power 10.6 @ 7 000
Fuel tank 6.7 l

Transmission:
Gears/Clutch 6/wmp

Electrical:
Ignition 6 v/6 Ah/magneto/D
Starting kick

Notes: KE 175 available.

Braking:
Front/Rear 130 mm dm/120 mm dm
Front tyres 2.75 × 21 trials
Rear tyres 3.50 × 18 trials

Suspension:
Front/Rear T/SA (5-pos.)

Dimensions:
Ground clearance 250 mm
Seat height 787 mm
Wheelbase 1 350 mm
Overall length 2 120 mm
Dry weight 98 kg

Performance:
Top speed 110 km/h (p)
Fuel consumption ...

Kawasaki

KH 100

Engine:
Type 2-str single
Bore × Stroke 49.5 × 51.8 mm
Capacity 99 cc
Compression ratio 7:1
Carburettors 1/19 mm Mikuni
Maximum power 11.5 @ 8 000
Fuel tank 10 l

Transmission:
Gears/Clutch 5/wmp

Electrical:
Ignition 6 v/magneto
Starting kick

Notes:

Braking:
Front/Rear 130 mm dm/110 mm dm
Front tyres 2.50 × 18 road
Rear tyres 2.75 × 18 road

Suspension:
Front/Rear T/SA (3-pos.)

Dimensions:
Ground clearance 160 mm
Seat height 762 mm
Wheelbase 1 225 mm
Overall length 1 900 mm
Dry weight 89 kg

Performance:
Top speed 115 km/h (p)
Fuel consumption 3.6 l/100 km (p)

Kawasaki

KM 90

Engine:
Type 2-str single
Bore × Stroke 47 × 51.8 mm
Capacity 89 cc
Compression ratio 6.8:1
Carburettors 1/19 mm Mikuni
Maximum power 66 @ 6 500
Fuel tank 6 l

Transmission:
Gears/Clutch 5/wmp

Electrical:
Ignition 6 v/4 Ah/magneto
Starting kick

Notes:

Braking:
Front/Rear 110 mm drums
Front tyres 2.50 × 16 road
Rear tyres 3.00 × 14 road

Suspension:
Front/Rear T/SA

Dimensions:
Ground clearance 160 mm
Seat height 711 mm
Wheelbase 1 100 mm
Overall length 1 730 mm
Dry weight 76 kg

Performance:
Top speed 93 km/h (p)
Fuel consumption 3.2 l/100 km (p)

Kawasaki

75 MT-1

Engine:
Type 2-str single
Bore × Stroke 46 × 44 mm
Capacity 73 cc
Compression ratio 6.7:1
Carburettors 1/19 mm Mikuni
Maximum power 4.2 @ 6 500
Fuel tank 3 l

Transmission:
Gears/Clutch 3/A

Electrical:
Ignition 6 v/magneto
Starting kick

Notes: Fitted with folding handlebars.

Braking:
Front/Rear 90 mm drums
Front tyres 3.50 × 8 trials
Rear tyres 3.50 × 8 trials

Suspension:
Front/Rear T/SA

Dimensions:
Ground clearance 155 mm
Seat height 710 mm
Wheelbase 965 mm
Overall length 1 350 mm
Dry weight 50 kg

Performance:
Top speed 65 km/h
Fuel consumption ...

Kreidler (West Germany)

Kreidler concentrates on the manufacture of 50 cc mopeds and lightweight motorcycles and its factory was set up in 1950. The company's international reputation has been gained on the race scene where the 50 cc grand prix racing bike which develops 18 bhp has been very fast and successful. Kreidler also holds an absolute world speed record for 50 cc engines of 225 km/h. The company's faith in the reliability of its product is reflected by the golden pin and performance plaque that it presents to Kreidler owners on completion of 100 000 km.

Head Office: Kreidler Werke GmbH, Fahrzeugwerke, 7014 Kornwestheim, West Germany.

UK Concessionaires: Kreidler Concessionaires, Ferndown Industrial Estate, Ferndown, Dorset.

Kreidler   Florett Sports

Engine:
Type   2-str horizontal single
Bore × Stroke   40 × 39.7 mm
Capacity   49 cc
Compression ratio   ...
Carburettors   1/14 mm Bing
Maximum power   6.25 @ 8 500
Fuel tank   12.5 l

Transmission:
Gears/Clutch   4/wmp

Electrical:
Ignition   6 v/magneto
Starting   pedals

Notes: Tourer version develops 4 bhp with top speed of 70 km/h.

Braking:
Front/Rear   160 mm drums
Front tyres   2.75 × 17 road
Rear tyres   2.75 × 17 road

Suspension:
Front/Rear   T/SA

Dimensions:
Ground clearance   200 mm
Seat height   800 mm
Wheelbase   1 220 mm
Overall length   1 880 mm
Dry weight   76 kg

Performance:
Top speed   90 km/h
Fuel consumption   3 l/100 km

KTM (Austria)

KTM is one of Austria's two motorcycle manufacturers and has been in production since the last war. KTM has been particularly successful with motocross and trials competitions and won the 250 MX world championship in 1974. The styling of its latest range of road models has been well-received and both the GP 125 and 50 cc de luxe are fitted with magnesium wheels still normally found on racing machines rather than production road bikes.

Head Office: KTM Motorfahrzeugbau KG, Kronfief & Trunkenpolz, 5230 Mattighoffen, Austria.

UK Concessionaires: KTM (UK), Oxford House, Portsmouth Road, Thames Ditton, Surrey KT7 OXQ

KTM   **250 GS**

Engine:
Type 2-str Sachs single
Bore × Stroke 71 × 62 mm
Capacity 246 cc
Compression ratio 8.9:1
Carburettors 1/36 mm Bing
Maximum power 34 @ 7 400
Fuel tank 10 l

Transmission:
Gears/Clutch 6/wmp

Electrical:
Ignition 6 v/ε
Starting kick

Notes: Range of enduro models from 100 GS to 400 GS.

Braking:
Front/Rear 180 mm drums
Front tyres 3.00 × 21 trials
Rear tyres 4.50 × 18 trials

Suspension:
Front/Rear T/SA

Dimensions:
Ground clearance 266 mm
Seat height 838 mm
Wheelbase 1 473 mm
Overall length 2 210 mm
Dry weight 109 kg

Performance:
Top speed ...
Fuel consumption ...

KTM
GP 50 De Luxe

Engine:
Type 2-str Sachs single
Bore×Stroke 38×42 mm
Capacity 47 cc
Compression ratio 9:1
Carburettors 1/17 mm Bing
Maximum power 4.3 @ 5 700
Fuel tank 10 l

Transmission:
Gears/Clutch 4/wmp

Electrical:
Ignition 6 v/magneto
Starting kick

Notes: GP 125RS is a 6-speed model with similar styling and 122 cc engine.

Braking:
Front/Rear 130 mm drums
Front tyres 2.50×17 road
Rear tyres 2.75×17 road

Suspension:
Front/Rear T/SA

Dimensions:
Ground clearance 266 mm
Seat height 781 mm
Wheelbase 1 245 mm
Overall length 1 854 mm
Dry weight 73 kg

Performance:
Top speed 65 km/h (p)
Fuel consumption ...

KTM
Comet 50RS

Engine:
Type 2-str Sachs single
Bore×Stroke 38×42 mm
Capacity 47 cc
Compression ratio 9:1
Carburettors 1/17 mm Bing
Maximum power 4.3 @ 5 700
Fuel tank 10 l

Transmission:
Gears/Clutch 4/wmp

Electrical:
Ignition 6 v/magneto
Starting kick

Notes: Comet cross model also available.

Braking:
Front/Rear 130 mm drums
Front tyres 2.50×17 road
Rear tyres 2.75×17 road

Suspension:
Front/Rear T/SA

Dimensions:
Ground clearance 266 mm
Seat height 800 mm
Wheelbase 1 245 mm
Overall length 1 879 mm
Dry weight 66 kg

Performance:
Top speed 65 km/h (p)
Fuel consumption ...

KTM
Automatic

Engine:
Type 2-str horizontal single
Bore×Stroke 38×42 mm
Capacity 47 cc
Compression ratio 8:1
Carburettors 1/12 mm Bing
Maximum power 1.8 @ 4 500
Fuel tank 3.5 l

Transmission:
Gears/Clutch single/A

Electrical:
Ignition 6 v/magneto
Starting pedal

Notes:

Braking:
Front/Rear 90 mm drums
Front tyres 2.25×21 road
Rear tyres 2.25×21 road

Suspension:
Front/Rear T/SA

Dimensions:
Ground clearance 222 mm
Seat height 800 mm
Wheelbase 1 118 mm
Overall length 1 702 mm
Dry weight 41 kg

Performance:
Top speed ...
Fuel consumption ...

Lambretta (Spain)

SERVETA

Lambretta was one of the world's best-known makes of scooter during the fifties' and sixties' scooter boom and they were made, under licence from Innocenti of Italy, in several other countries. During the late 1960s, with sales declining and the company involved in serious industrial relations difficulties, it was bought up by British Leyland who proceeded to sell the scooter operation and concentrate production on the Innocenti Mini. Lambretta production was then switched to Spain where scooters were already being assembled under licence by Serveta. The current range of Serveta Lambretta also includes the 125 cc Scooterlinea.

Head Office: Serveta Industrial S.A., Avenida de Bilbao, 3, 716040 Eibar, Spain.
UK Concessionaires: Lambretta Scooters, 87 Beddington Lane, Croydon CRO 4TD.

Lambretta **Jet 200**

Engine:
Type 2-str horizontal single
Bore × Stroke 66 × 58 mm
Capacity 198 cc
Compression ratio 7:1
Carburettors 1/20 mm Dell'Orto
Maximum power 9.75 hp
Fuel tank 8.5 l

Transmission:
Gears/Clutch 4/wmp

Electrical:
Ignition 6 v/magneto
Starting kick

Notes: TL = trailing link front suspension.

Braking:
Front/Rear 180 mm dm/200 mm dm
Front tyres 3.50 × 10 road
Rear tyres 3.50 × 10 road

Suspension:
Front/Rear TL/shockers

Dimensions:
Ground clearance 165 mm
Seat height 810 mm
Wheelbase 1 290 mm
Overall length 1800 mm
Dry weight 123 kg

Performance:
Top speed 107 km/h
Fuel consumption 3.05 l/100 km

Lambretta — Special 150

Engine:
Type 2-str horizontal single
Bore × Stroke ...
Capacity 148 cc
Compression ratio 7:1
Carburettors 1/18 mm Dell'Orto
Maximum power 7.6 hp
Fuel tank 8.5 l

Transmission:
Gears/Clutch 4/wmp

Electrical:
Ignition 6 v/magneto
Starting kick

Notes:

Braking:
Front/Rear 180 mm dm/200 mm dm
Front tyres 3.50×10 road
Rear tyres 3.50×10 road

Suspension:
Front/Rear TL/shockers

Dimensions:
Ground clearance 165 mm
Seat height 810 mm
Wheelbase 1 290 mm
Overall length 1 800 mm
Dry weight ...

Performance:
Top speed 97 km/h
Fuel consumption 2.80 l/100 km

Lambretta Sony 200

Laverda (Italy)

1000 3/C

Engine:
Type 4-str dohc triple
Bore×Stroke 75×74 mm
Capacity 980.76 cc
Compression ratio 9:1
Carburettors 3/32 mm Dell'Orto
Maximum power 80 @ 7 250
Fuel tank 20 l

Transmission:
Gears/Clutch 5/wmp

Electrical:
Ignition 12 v/27 Ah/ε/A
Starting electric

Notes:

Braking:
Front/Rear 280 mm dc/230 mm dm
Front tyres 4.10×18 road
Rear tyres 4.10×18 road

Suspension:
Front/Rear T/SA (3-pos.)

Dimensions:
Ground clearance 140 mm
Seat height 800 mm
Wheelbase 1 486 mm
Overall length 2 180 mm
Dry weight 214 kg

Performance:
Top speed 215 km/h
Fuel consumption 6.5 l/100 km

Laverda

750 SFC

Engine:
Type 4-str sohc twin
Bore×Stroke 80×74 mm
Capacity 743.92 cc
Compression ratio 9.8:1
Carburettors 2/36 mm Dell'Orto
Maximum power 75 @ 7 500
Fuel tank 25 l

Transmission:
Gears/Clutch 5/wmp

Electrical:
Ignition 12 v/18 Ah/b&c/D
Starting electric

Notes:

Braking:
Front/Rear 280 mm discs
Front tyres 4.00×18 road
Rear tyres 4.00×18 road

Suspension:
Front/Rear T/SA (3-pos.)

Dimensions:
Ground clearance 140 mm
Seat height 800 mm
Wheelbase 1 465 mm
Overall length 2 200 mm
Dry weight 210 kg

Performance:
Top speed 215 km/h
Fuel consumption 7.5 l/100 km

Laverda

750 SF2

Engine:
Type 4-str sohc twin
Bore×Stroke 80×74 mm
Capacity 743.92 cc
Compression ratio 8.9:1
Carburettors 2/36 mm Dell'Orto
Maximum power 65 @ 7 000
Fuel tank 19 l

Transmission:
Gears/Clutch 5/wmp

Electrical:
Ignition 12 v/18 Ah/b&c/D
Starting electric

Notes: GTL model develops 53 bhp with top speed of 185 km/h.

Braking:
Front/Rear 280 mm dc/230 mm dm
Front tyres 3.50×18 road
Rear tyres 4.00×18 road

Suspension:
Front/Rear T/SA (3-pos.)

Dimensions:
Ground clearance 140 mm
Seat height 800 mm
Wheelbase 1 465 mm
Overall length 2 200 mm
Dry weight 218 kg

Performance:
Top speed 195 km/h
Fuel consumption 7 l/100 km

Laverda 250

Engine:
Type 2-str single
Bore × Stroke 68 × 68 mm
Capacity 246.95 cc
Compression ratio 10:1
Carburettors 1/32 mm Dell'Orto
Maximum power 37 @ 7 000
Fuel tank 11 l

Transmission:
Gears/Clutch 5/dmp

Electrical:
Ignition 12 v/6 Ah/ε/A
Starting kick

Notes: Fork rake adjustable 3 ways.

Braking:
Front/Rear 180 mm drums
Front tyres 3.00 × 21 trials
Rear tyres 4.00 × 18 trials

Suspension:
Front/Rear T/SA

Dimensions:
Ground clearance 200 mm
Seat height 800 mm
Wheelbase 1 465 mm
Overall length 2 086 mm
Dry weight 108 kg

Performance:
Top speed 130 km/h
Fuel consumption 5 l/100 km

 The family-owned Laverda industrial group began in 1873 when Pietro Laverda founded an agricultural machinery factory at Breganze 20 km north of Vicenza, Italy. The group today also runs a caravan company and several foundries as well as Moto Laverda which was started in 1949. The new Laverda factory was completed in 1973 and a staff of 250 produce about 8 000 bikes annually, half of which are exported to Europe, North America and Australia. At first Laverda produced small 4-stroke singles and in the sixties made a popular 2-stroke moped. The large twins were launched in 1968 and since then have been very successful in long-distance road racing.
Head Office: Moto Laverda S.p.A., 36042 Breganze, Vicenza, Italy.
UK Concessionaires: Slater Bros, Collington, near Bromyard, Herefordshire.

Maico (West Germany)

The Maico company was started by the brothers Otto and Wilhelm Maisch in 1934 and their first motorcycle was a 100 cc road bike with Ilo engine. During World War II Maico moved to Pfäffingen and produced parts for the German air-force. By 1950 the company was again in serious production and the range included a 400 cc twin and the big Maicoletta touring scooters. For a while in the fifties Maico assembled cars using 2-stroke Heinkel engines, and the power and reliability of the cross-country models led to the German Federal forces choosing the M250 for army use and some 10 000 machines were eventually delivered. Maico off-road bikes have been well-received in the USA market and they have been particularly successful in the 250 and 500 cc moto-cross world championships and all forms of trials competitions.

Head Office: Maico-Fahrzeugfabrik GmbH, 7403 Ammerbuch-Pfäffingen 2. West Germany.

UK Concessionaires: Bryan Goss Motor Cycles, 31, Vincents Street, Yeovil, Somerset.

Maico — MD 250

Engine:
Type 2-str rotary valve single
Bore × Stroke 76 × 54 mm
Capacity 245 cc
Compression ratio 12:1
Carburettors 1/32 mm Bing
Maximum power 27 @ 7 800
Fuel tank 12.5 l

Transmission:
Gears/Clutch 6/wmp

Electrical:
Ignition 12 v/ε/A
Starting kick

Notes:

Braking:
Front/Rear 180 mm dm/160 mm dm
Front tyres 2.75 × 18 road
Rear tyres 3.25 × 18 road

Suspension:
Front/Rear T/SA (3-pos.)

Dimensions:
Ground clearance 178 mm
Seat height 736 mm
Wheelbase 1 372 mm
Overall length 1 830 mm
Dry weight 120 kg

Performance:
Top speed 150 km/h
Fuel consumption ...

Maico

MD 125 Supersport

Engine:
Type 2-str rotary valve single
Bore×Stroke 54×54
Capacity 124 cc
Compression ratio 11:1
Carburettors 1/26 mm Bing
Maximum power 16 @ 7 800
Fuel tank 13.5 l

Transmission:
Gears/Clutch 6/wmp

Electrical:
Ignition 6 v/magneto
Starting kick

Notes: RS 125, a racing version, exceeds 200 km/h.

Braking:
Front/Rear 136 mm drums
Front tyres 2.50×16 road
Rear tyres 3.00×16 road

Suspension:
Front/Rear T/SA

Dimensions:
Ground clearance 178 mm
Seat height 736 mm
Wheelbase 1 372 mm
Overall length 1 830 mm
Dry weight 99 kg

Performance:
Top speed 123 km/h
Fuel consumption ...

Maico

MD 50 Sport

Engine:
Type 2-str rotary valve single
Bore×Stroke 38×44 mm
Capacity 49 cc
Compression ratio 11.2:1
Carburettors 1/20 mm Bing
Maximum power 6.3 @ 8 200
Fuel tank 13.5 l

Transmission:
Gears/Clutch 6/wmp

Electrical:
Ignition 6 v/magneto
Starting kick

Notes:

Braking:
Front/Rear 136 mm drums
Front tyres 2.50×16 road
Rear tyres 3.00×16 road

Suspension:
Front/Rear T/SA

Dimensions:
Ground clearance 178 mm
Seat height 736 mm
Wheelbase 1 372 mm
Overall length 1 830 mm
Dry weight 91 kg

Performance:
Top speed 93 km/h
Fuel consumption ...

Maico

GS 400

Engine:
Type 2-str single
Bore×Stroke 77×83 mm
Capacity 386 cc
Compression ratio 10:1
Carburettors 1/36 mm Bing
Maximum power 41 @ 6 500
Fuel tank 16 l

Transmission:
Gears/Clutch 4/wmp

Electrical:
Ignition 6 v/8 Ah/magneto
Starting kick

Notes: 125 and 250 cc versions and full range of moto-cross models.

Braking:
Front/Rear 136 mm dm/160 mm dm
Front tyres 3.00×21 trials
Rear tyres 4.50×18 trials

Suspension:
Front/Rear T/SA

Dimensions:
Ground clearance 220 mm
Seat height 863 mm
Wheelbase 1 400 mm
Overall length ...
Dry weight 110 kg

Performance:
Top speed ...
Fuel consumption ...

Malaguti (Italy)

Monte

Engine:
Type 2-str Morini single
Bore × Stroke 39 × 41.8 mm
Capacity 49.93 cc
Compression ratio 9.6:1
Carburettors 1/19 mm Dell'Orto
Maximum power 6.5 @ 8 500
Fuel tank 6.8 l

Transmission:
Gears/Clutch 5/wmp

Electrical:
Ignition 6 v/magneto
Starting pedal

Notes:

Braking:
Front/Rear 120 mm drums
Front tyres 2.50 × 19 trials
Rear tyres 3.00 × 17 trials

Suspension:
Front/Rear T/SA (3-pos.)

Dimensions:
Ground clearance 222 mm
Seat height 825 mm
Wheelbase 1 290 mm
Overall length 1 981 mm
Dry weight 72 kg

Performance:
Top speed 72 km/h
Fuel consumption ...

Malaguti

Olympique

Engine:
Type 2-str Morini single
Bore × Stroke 39 × 41.8 mm
Capacity 49.93 cc
Compression ratio 9.6:1
Carburettors 1/19 mm Dell'Orto
Maximum power 6.5 @ 8 500
Fuel tank 11.3 l

Transmission:
Gears/Clutch 4/5/wmp

Electrical:
Ignition 6 v/magneto
Starting pedal

Notes: Superquattro 4-speed model has similar specification.

Braking:
Front/Rear 120 mm drums
Front tyres 2.25 × 18 road
Rear tyres 2.50 × 18 road

Suspension:
Front/Rear T/SA

Dimensions:
Ground clearance 140 mm
Seat height 745 mm
Wheelbase 1 168 mm
Overall length 1 790 mm
Dry weight 64 kg

Performance:
Top speed 88 km/h
Fuel consumption ...

Malaguti

Hombre

Engine:
Type 2-str Morini single
Bore × Stroke 39 × 41.8 mm
Capacity 49.93 cc
Compression ratio 9.6:1
Carburettors 1/19 mm Dell'Orto
Maximum power 6.5 @ 8 500
Fuel tank 11 l

Transmission:
Gears/Clutch 4/wmp

Electrical:
Ignition 6 v/magneto
Starting pedal

Notes:

Braking:
Front/Rear 120 mm drums
Front tyres 2.25 × 18 road
Rear tyres 2.50 × 18 road

Suspension:
Front/Rear T/SA

Dimensions:
Ground clearance 140 mm
Seat height 745 mm
Wheelbase 1 168 mm
Overall length 1 790 mm
Dry weight 68 kg

Performance:
Top speed 88 km/h
Fuel consumption ...

Malaguti   **Mon Ami**

Engine:
Type 2-str horizontal single
Bore × Stroke 39 × 42 mm
Capacity 47.6 cc
Compression ratio 6.5:1
Carburettors 1/14 mm Dell'Orto
Maximum power 2 @ 5 500
Fuel tank 3.4 l

Transmission:
Gears/Clutch single/A

Electrical:
Ignition 6 v/magneto
Starting pedal

Notes: 2-speed version also available.

Braking:
Front/Rear 90 mm drums
Front tyres 2.25 × 16 road
Rear tyres 2.25 × 16 road

Suspension:
Front/Rear T/SA

Dimensions:
Ground clearance 133 mm
Seat height 770 mm
Wheelbase 1 028 mm
Overall length 1 575 mm
Dry weight 31 kg

Performance:
Top speed 56 km/h
Fuel consumption ...

Malaguti is the third largest moped producer in Italy and was founded in 1937 by the Malaguti family which still controls the company in Bologna, northern Italy. Malaguti is closely associated with the Franco Morini Company of Casalecchio di Reno which specializes in the construction of moped and light motorcycle engines. All the Malaguti range are fitted with Morini engines. Malaguti exports widely in Europe, the Middle East and North America. Its complete range of twelve models includes an off-road fun bike designed specifically for children.

Head Office: Malaguti S.p.A. 40068 S. Lazzaro di Savena (BO), Italy.
UK Concessionaires: Malaguti UK, High Street, Ripley, Surrey GU23 6AF.

Montesa (Spain)

Montesa is Spain's first and largest motorcycle manufacturer. The firm's origins can be traced to a small workshop in Barcelona started by Sr Pedro Permanyer-Puigjaner in 1941. The fifties were a difficult time but in 1962 a new plant was opened where the latest mass-production techniques were used to produce motorcycles, engines and light outboard motors. Montesa's reputation is firmly based on its wide range of moto-cross and trials machines which have won many international competitions. Technically the company has contributed a good deal in its experience of and research into suspension problems, and its bikes are in world-wide demand. A selection of Montesa's 50 cc range is given on page 114.

Head Office: Permanyer, SA de Industrias Mecanicas, Avda. Virgen de la Paloma, 21–53, Esplugas de Llobregat (Barcelona), Spain.

UK Concessionaires: Jim Sandiford (Imports) Ltd, 30/38 Walmersley Road, Bury, Lancs BL9 6DP.

Montesa — King Scorpion 250

Engine:
Type   2-str single
Bore × Stroke   70 × 64 mm
Capacity   246.3 cc
Compression ratio   10:1
Carburettors   1/32 mm Bing
Maximum power   26 @ 6 500
Fuel tank   10 l

Transmission:
Gears/Clutch   5/wmp

Electrical:
Ignition   6 v/8 Ah/ε/A
Starting   kick

Notes: Also as Rapita 250 road machine. Fitted with oil injection.

Braking:
Front/Rear   130 mm dm/150 mm dm
Front tyres   3.00 × 21 trials
Rear tyres   4.00 × 18 trials

Suspension:
Front/Rear   T/SA (2-pos.)

Dimensions:
Ground clearance   250 mm
Seat height   930 mm
Wheelbase   1 425 mm
Overall length   2 130 mm
Dry weight   110 kg

Performance:
Top speed   140 km/h
Fuel consumption   …

Montesa

Cota 247 T

Engine:
Type   2-str single
Bore × Stroke   72·5 × 60 mm
Capacity   247.7 cc
Compression ratio   10.1
Carburettors   1/27 mm Amal
Maximum power   20 @ 7 000
Fuel tank   8.1 l

Transmission:
Gears/Clutch   5/wmp

Electrical:
Ignition   6 v/magneto
Starting   kick

Notes:

Braking:
Front/Rear   110 mm drums
Front tyres   2.75 × 21 trials
Rear tyres   4.00 × 21 trials

Suspension:
Front/Rear   T/SA (2 pos.)

Dimensions:
Ground clearance   250 mm
Seat height   760 mm
Wheelbase   1 325 mm
Overall length   2 035 mm
Dry weight   91 kg

Performance:
Top speed   105 km/h
Fuel consumption   4.6 l/100 km

Montesa

Cota 172

Engine:
Type   2-str single
Bore × Stroke   60.9 × 54 mm
Capacity   162 cc
Compression ratio   11.5:1
Carburettors   1/20 mm Amal
Maximum power   15 @ 7 000
Fuel tank   4.5 l

Transmission:
Gears/Clutch   6/wmp

Electrical:
Ignition   6 v/magneto
Starting   kick

Notes: Also 123 T producing 13 bhp

Braking:
Front/Rear   110 mm drums
Front tyres   2.75 × 21 trials
Rear tyres   4.00 × 18 trials

Suspension:
Front/Rear   T/SA

Dimensions:
Ground clearance   295 mm
Seat height   736 mm
Wheelbase   1 270 mm
Overall length   1 930 mm
Dry weight   78 kg

Performance:
Top speed   96 km/h
Fuel consumption   4.6 l/100 km

Montesa

Cota 25c

Engine:
Type   2-str single
Bore × Stroke   38 × 43 mm
Capacity   48.7 cc
Compression ratio   9:1
Carburettors   1/14 mm Bing
Maximum power   1.6 hp
Fuel tank   4.5 l

Transmission:
Gears/Clutch   3/wmp

Electrical:
Ignition   6 v/magneto
Starting   kick

Notes: Also with automatic gearbox.

Braking:
Front/Rear   100 mm drums
Front tyres   2.00 × 16 trials
Rear tyres   2.50 × 15 trials

Suspension:
Front/Rear   T/SA

Dimensions:
Ground clearance   240 mm
Seat height   560 mm
Wheelbase   940 mm
Overall length   1 500 mm
Dry weight   35 kg

Performance:
Top speed   40 km/h
Fuel consumption   1.7 l/100 km

Montesa — Rapita 50 48.7 cc 2-stroke roadster

Montesa — Cota 49 3-speed trial bike

Montesa — Mini Montesa 50 cc automatic moped

Motobecane (France)

Motobecane and Motoconfort were created separately in the early twenties but in 1930 combined and the company is now the world's largest manufacturer of mopeds and bicycles. Between the wars 500 and 750 cc fours were built but for some years now the Saint-Quentin assembly factory has concentrated on small 2-strokes. In 1949 the famous Mobylette range was launched, of which more than 11 million have since been made. Motobecane has always offered an extremely wide range of models powered by their own 50 cc engine built at the Polymecanique engine plant in Pantin. In 1970 production of a 125 cc twin began, followed by the 350 triple; and the latest model is a 500 cc 2-stroke triple with electronic fuel injection claimed to develop 55 bhp. In 1972 the moped range was restyled with the introduction of the Mobyx models. About a third of production is exported and licences have been granted to countries like Spain, Iran, Zaire and Morocco.

Head Office: Motobecane, 16, Rue Lesault – 93502 Pantin, France.
UK Concessionaires: Motor Imports Co. Ltd, 700 Purley Way, Croydon CR9 4QX.

Motobecane Motoconfort 350

Engine:
Type 2-str triple
Bore × Stroke 53 × 52.8 mm
Capacity 349 cc
Compression ratio 10:1
Carburettors 3/24 mm Gurtner
Maximum power 38 @ 7 200
Fuel tank 19 l

Transmission:
Gears/Clutch 5/wmp

Electrical:
Ignition 12 v/9 Ah/ε/A
Starting kick

Notes:

Braking:
Front/Rear 275 mm dc/180 mm dm
Front tyres 3.00 × 18 road
Rear tyres 3.50 × 18 road

Suspension:
Front/Rear T/SA (3-pos.)

Dimensions:
Ground clearance ...
Seat height ...
Wheelbase 1 330 mm
Overall length 2 050 mm
Dry weight 170 kg

Performance:
Top speed 165 km/h
Fuel consumption 8 l/100 km

Mobylette by Motobecane — X7S

Engine:
Type 2-str single
Bore×Stroke 39×41.8 mm
Capacity 49.9 cc
Compression ratio 8:1
Carburettors 1/7 mm Gurtner
Maximum power 1.8 @ 5 500
Fuel tank 3.6 l

Transmission:
Gears/Clutch single/A

Electrical:
Ignition 6 v/magneto
Starting pedal

Notes: X1 is a smaller version with folding handlebars, and detuned engine.

Braking:
Front/Rear 82 mm drums
Front tyres 2.75×10 road
Rear tyres 2.75×10 road

Suspension:
Front/Rear T/Saddle

Dimensions:
Ground clearance 127 mm
Seat height 685 mm
Wheelbase 990 mm
Overall length 1 460 mm
Dry weight 38 kg

Performance:
Top speed 48 km/h
Fuel consumption 2.1 l/100 km

Mobylette by Motobecane — Sports 50

Engine:
Type 2-str single
Bore×Stroke 39×41.8 mm
Capacity 49.9 cc
Compression ratio 8.8:1
Carburettors 1/7 mm Gurtner
Maximum power 2.5 @ 5 500
Fuel tank 8 l

Transmission:
Gears/Clutch single/A

Electrical:
Ignition 6v/magneto
Starting pedal

Notes: Also in Sports Speciale form with swept-up exhaust.

Braking:
Front/Rear 101 mm drums
Front tyres 2.50×17 road
Rear tyres 2.50×17 road

Suspension:
Front/Rear T/SA

Dimensions:
Ground clearance 127 mm
Seat height 787 mm
Wheelbase 1 194 mm
Overall length 1 753 mm
Dry weight 57 kg

Performance:
Top speed 56 km/h
Fuel consumption 2.1 l/100 km

Mobylette by Motobecane — Mastermatic

Engine:
Type 2-str single
Bore×Stroke 39×41.8 mm
Capacity 49.9 cc
Compression ratio 8.8:1
Carburettors 1/7 mm Gurtner
Maximum power 2.5 @ 5 500
Fuel tank 7.9 l

Transmission:
Gears/Clutch single/A

Electrical:
Ignition 6v/magneto
Starting pedal

Notes: Luxamatic model also available.

Braking:
Front/Rear 101 mm drums
Front tyres 2.25×18 road
Rear tyres 2.25×18 road

Suspension:
Front/Rear T/SA

Dimensions:
Ground clearance 127 mm
Seat height 787 mm
Wheelbase 1 194 mm
Overall length 1 828 mm
Dry weight 56 kg

Performance:
Top speed 56 km/h
Fuel consumption 2.1 l/100 km

Mobylette by Motobecane

Commuter

Engine:
Type 2-str single
Bore × Stroke 39 × 41.8 mm
Capacity 49.9 cc
Compression ratio 8:1
Carburettors 1/7 mm Gurtner
Maximum power 1.5 @ 4 500
Fuel tank 2.3 l

Transmission:
Gears/Clutch single/A

Electrical:
Ignition 6 v/magneto
Starting pedal

Notes: Known in France as the Cady.

Braking:
Front/Rear 70 mm drums
Front tyres 2.00 × 16 road
Rear tyres 2.00 × 16 road

Suspension:
Front/Rear T/SA

Dimensions:
Ground clearance 127 mm
Seat height 787 mm
Wheelbase 1 016 mm
Overall length 1 524 mm
Dry weight 35 kg

Performance:
Top speed 40 km/h
Fuel consumption 2 l/100 km

Mobylette by Motobecane

Mono 50

Engine:
Type 2-str single
Bore × Stroke 39 × 41.8 mm
Capacity 49.9 cc
Compression ratio 8.8:1
Carburettors 1/7 mm Gurtner
Maximum power 1.8 @ 5 500
Fuel tank 4 l

Transmission:
Gears/Clutch single/A

Electrical:
Ignition 6 v/magneto
Starting pedal

Notes: Also made with dual seat.

Braking:
Front/Rear 82 mm drums
Front tyres 2.25 × 17 road
Rear tyres 2.25 × 17 road

Suspension:
Front/Rear T/SA

Dimensions:
Ground clearance 127 mm
Seat height 787 mm
Wheelbase 1 143 mm
Overall length 1 753 mm
Dry weight 48 kg

Performance:
Top speed 56 km/h
Fuel consumption 2.1 l/100 km

Mobylette by Motobecane

Majormatic

Engine:
Type 2-str single
Bore × Stroke 39 × 41.8 mm
Capacity 49.9 cc
Compression ratio 8.8:1
Carburettors 1/7 mm Gurtner
Maximum power 1.8 @ 5 500
Fuel tank 4 l

Transmission:
Gears/Clutch variable/A

Electrical:
Ignition 6 v/magneto
Starting pedal

Notes: Majorette is single speed version.

Braking:
Front/Rear 70 mm dm/82 mm dm
Front tyres 2.00 × 17 road
Rear tyres 2.00 × 17 road

Suspension:
Front/Rear T/rigid

Dimensions:
Ground clearance 127 mm
Seat height 762 mm
Wheelbase 1 118 mm
Overall length 1 676 mm
Dry weight 43 kg

Performance:
Top speed 56 km/h
Fuel consumption 2.1 l/100 km

Moto Guzzi (Italy)

V1000 1-Convert

Engine:
Type 4-str vee-twin
Bore × Stroke 88 × 78 mm
Capacity 949 cc
Compression ratio 9.2:1
Carburettors 2/30 mm Dell'Orto
Maximum power 71 @ 6 500
Fuel tank 25 l

Transmission:
Gears/Clutch 2/sdp

Electrical:
Ignition 12 v/32 Ah/b/c/A
Starting electric

Notes: Hydraulic converter transmission and integral brake system fitted.

Braking:
Front/Rear 300 mm dc/240 mm dc
Front tyres 4.10 × 18 road
Rear tyres 4.10 × 18 road

Suspension:
Front/Rear T/SA (5-pos.)

Dimensions:
Ground clearance 178 mm
Seat height 819 mm
Wheelbase 1 486 mm
Overall length 2 210 mm
Dry weight 240 kg

Performance:
Top speed 170 km/h
Fuel consumption 6 l/100 km

Moto Guzzi

850-T3 California

Engine:
Type 4-str ohv vee-twin
Bore × Stroke 83 × 78 mm
Capacity 844 cc
Compression ratio 9.5:1
Carburettors 2/30 mm Dell'Orto
Maximum power 68 @ 7 000*
Fuel tank 24 l

Transmission:
Gears/Clutch 5/sdp

Electrical:
Ignition 12 v/32 Ah/b/c/A
Starting electric (no kick)

Notes: Fitted integral brake system. Standard model also available.

Braking:
Front/Rear 300 mm dc/240 mm dc
Front tyres 3.50 × 18 road
Rear tyres 4.10 × 18 road

Suspension:
Front/Rear T/SA (5-pos.)

Dimensions:
Ground clearance 190 mm
Seat height 812 mm
Wheelbase 1 498 mm
Overall length 2 260 mm
Dry weight 225 kg

Performance:
Top speed 195 km/h
Fuel consumption 6 l/100 km

Moto Guzzi

750-S3

Engine:
Type 4-str ohv vee-twin
Bore × Stroke 82.5 × 70.2 mm
Capacity 748 cc
Compression ratio 10:1
Carburettors 2/30 mm Dell'Orto
Maximum power 70 @ 7 000*
Fuel tank 22 l

Transmission:
Gears/Clutch 5/sdp

Electrical:
Ignition 12 v/32 Ah/b/c/A
Starting electric

Notes: Integral brake system and Guzzi shaft drive fitted.

Braking:
Front/Rear 300 mm dc/240 mm dc
Front tyres 3.25 × 18 road
Rear tyres 3.50 × 18 road

Suspension:
Front/Rear T/SA (3-pos.)

Dimensions:
Ground clearance 150 mm
Seat height 800 mm
Wheelbase 1 473 mm
Overall length 2 197 mm
Dry weight 206 kg

Performance:
Top speed 206 km/h
Fuel consumption 6 l/100 km

Moto Guzzi

Falconé

Engine:
Type 4-str horizontal single
Bore × Stroke 80 × 82 mm
Capacity 499 cc
Compression 7:1
Carburettors 1/29 mm Dell'Orto
Maximum power 27 @ 4 800*
Fuel tank 18 l

Transmission:
Gears/Clutch 4/wmp

Electrical:
Ignition 12 v/18 Ah/b&c/D
Starting kick

Notes: Army and police bike features quiet double exhaust pipe.

Braking:
Front/Rear 180 mm drums
Front tyres 3.50 × 18 road
Rear tyres 3.50 × 18 road

Suspension:
Front/Rear T/SA (3-pos.)

Dimensions:
Ground clearance 160 mm
Seat height 813 mm
Wheelbase 1 450 mm
Overall length 2 170 mm
Dry weight 214 kg

Performance:
Top speed 130 km/h
Fuel consumption 4 l/100 km

Moto Guzzi

350 GTS

Engine:
Type 4-str sohc four
Bore × Stroke 50 × 44 mm
Capacity 345.5 cc
Compression ratio 10:1
Carburettors 4/20 mm Dell'Orto
Maximum power 38 @ 9 500*
Fuel tank 17 l

Transmission:
Gears/Clutch 5/wmp

Electrical:
Ignition 12 v/12 Ah/b&c/A
Starting electric

Notes: Also 400 GTS model developing 40 bhp.

Braking:
Front/Rear 180 mm dm/160 mm dm
Front tyres 3.00 × 18 road
Rear tyres 3.25 × 18 road

Suspension:
Front/Rear T/SA (3-pos.)

Dimensions:
Ground clearance 180 mm
Seat height 762 mm
Wheelbase 1 308 mm
Overall length 1 829 mm
Dry weight 168 kg

Performance:
Top speed 160 km/h
Fuel consumption 6.8 l/100 km

Moto Guzzi

250 TS

Engine:
Type 2-str twin
Bore × Stroke 56 × 47 mm
Capacity 231.4 cc
Compression ratio 10:1
Carburettors 2/25 mm Dell'Orto
Maximum power 30 @ 7 400*
Fuel tank 13.5 l

Transmission:
Gears/Clutch 5/wmp

Electrical:
Ignition 6 v/9 Ah/ε/A
Starting kick

Notes:

Braking:
Front/Rear 180 mm dm/160 mm dm
Front tyres 3.00 × 18 road
Rear tyres 3.25 × 18 road

Suspension:
Front/Rear T/SA (3-pos.)

Dimensions:
Ground clearance 178 mm
Seat height 762 mm
Wheelbase 1 308 mm
Overall length 1 829 mm
Dry weight 129 kg

Performance:
Top speed 150 km/h
Fuel consumption 7 l/100 km

Moto Guzzi   2-str 49 cc Nibbio (also in Cross version)

Moto Guzzi   2-str 49 cc Chiù (Dingo model also available)

MOTO GUZZI Since 1967 Moto Guzzi has been run by the Società Esercizio Industrie Moto Meccaniche (SEIMM) following financial difficulties during the mid-sixties' motorcycle recession.
Famous for big bikes, Moto Guzzi has been reorganized under its president Alejandro De Tomaso and produces some 85 000 mopeds, motorcycles and three-wheeled transport vehicles a year, of which half is exported. Moto Guzzi bikes are widely used by the police and armed forces from Albania to the USA. The company was originally founded in 1921 by Carlo Guzzi and Georgio Parodi and early machines were 500 cc flat singles with ohv. Until 1957 Moto Guzzi was very active in road racing and has won 14 world championship titles. Its interesting designs, often wind-tunnel tested, have resulted in many legendary models like the 500 cc vee-eight which developed 80 bhp and a top speed of 280 km/h.
Head Office: SEIMM Moto Guzzi S.p.A., 22054 Mandello del Lario (Como), Italy.
UK Concessionaires: Moto Guzzi, 21 Crawley Road, Luton, Beds.

Moto Morini (Italy)

The 3½ Sport and Strada Morinis come from a small Italian factory that was founded in 1937 for the production of motor cars and delivery tricycles. Since 1946 the factory has specialized in 2-stroke mopeds (the Corsarino range) and 4-stroke lightweights in street and enduro form (the Corsaro models). The 350 twins are top of the range but the company also makes the Corsaro Special which is a 5-speed single of 150 cc capacity and capable of 140 km/h.

Head Office: Fabbrica Italiana Motocicli di Gabriella Morini, 40133 Bologna – via A. Bergami 7, Italy.
UK Concessionaires: Harglo Ltd, 462 Station Road, Dorridge, Solihull, Warwicks.

Moto Morini 3½ Sport

Engine:
Type   4-str ohv vee-twin
Bore × Stroke   62 × 57 mm
Capacity   344 cc
Compression ratio   11:1
Carburettors   2/25 mm Dell'Orto
Maximum power   42 @ 8 500*
Fuel tank   14 l

Transmission:
Gears/Clutch   6/dmp

Electrical:
Ignition   12 v/9 Ah/ε/A
Starting   kick

Notes: Strada roadster version develops 39 bhp*.

Braking:
Front/Rear 230 mm dm/180 mm dm
Front tyres   3.25 × 18 road
Rear tyres   4.10 × 18 road

Suspension:
Front/Rear   T/SA (3-pos.)

Dimensions:
Ground clearance   229 mm
Seat height   762 mm
Wheelbase   1 390 mm
Overall length   2 060 mm
Dry weight   144 kg

Performance:
Top speed   175 km/h
Fuel consumption   4.3 l/100 km

Mototrans (Spain)

350 Vento

Engine:
Type 4-str ohc single
Bore × Stroke 75×75 mm
Capacity 340 cc
Compression ratio 9.5:1
Carburettors 1/32 mm Amal
Maximum power 32 @ 6 500
Fuel tank 16 l

Transmission:
Gears/Clutch 5/wmp

Electrical:
Ignition 12v/14Ah/b&c/A
Starting kick

Notes: Also 350 cc Scrambler, Road and Policia model versions.

Braking:
Front/Rear 230 mm dc/160 dm
Front tyres 3.25×18 road
Rear tyres 4.00×18 road

Suspension:
Front/Rear T/SA (3-pos.)

Dimensions:
Ground clearance ...
Seat height 750 mm
Wheelbase 1 370 mm
Overall length 2 010 mm
Dry weight 120 kg

Performance:
Top speed 160 km/h
Fuel consumption 5 l/100 km

Mototrans

300 Forza

Engine:
Type 4-str ohc single
Bore × Stroke 66×75 mm
Capacity 299.8 cc
Compression ratio 9:1
Carburettors 1/30 mm Amal
Maximum power 26 @ 6 500
Fuel tank 12 l

Transmission:
Gears/Clutch 5/wmp

Electrical:
Ignition 12 v/14 Ah/b&c/A
Starting electric

Notes:

Braking:
Front/Rear 230 mm dc/160 mm dm
Front tyres 3.25×18 road
Rear tyres 4.00×18 road

Suspension:
Front/Rear T/SA

Dimensions:
Ground clearance ...
Seat height 785 mm
Wheelbase 1 355 mm
Overall length 2 050 mm
Dry weight 130 kg

Performance:
Top speed 130 km/h
Fuel consumption 4 l/100 km

Mototrans

250 Road

Engine:
Type 4-str sohc single
Bore × Stroke 69×61 mm
Capacity 246 cc
Compression ratio 10:1
Carburettors 1/27 mm Amal
Maximum power 25 @ 6 500
Fuel tank 9 l

Transmission:
Gears/Clutch 5/wmp

Electrical:
Ignition 12 v/14 Ah/b&c/A
Starting kick

Notes:

Braking:
Front/Rear 180 mm drums
Front tyres 3.25×18 road
Rear tyres 4.00×18 road

Suspension:
Front/Rear T/SA

Dimensions:
Ground clearance ...
Seat height 750 mm
Wheelbase 1 360 mm
Overall length 2 040 mm
Dry weight 122 kg

Performance:
Top speed 120 km/h
Fuel consumption 4 l/100 km

Mototrans 50TS

Engine:
Type 2-str single
Bore×Stroke 38.8×41.3 mm
Capacity 49.6 cc
Compression ratio 11.2:1
Carburettors 1/14 mm Amal
Maximum power 2.2 @ 5 200
Fuel tank 7 l

Transmission:
Gears/Clutch 4/wmp

Electrical:
Ignition 6 v/magneto
Starting kick

Notes: Also Serda (73 cc) and Pronto (97.6 cc) models.

Braking:
Front/Rear 95 mm dm/110 mm dm
Front tyres 2.25×18 road
Rear tyres 2.50×17 road

Suspension:
Front/Rear T/SA

Dimensions:
Ground clearance ...
Seat height 750 mm
Wheelbase 1 200 mm
Overall length 1 920 mm
Dry weight 55 kg

Performance:
Top speed 40 km/h
Fuel consumption 2 l/100 km

Mototrans has been producing Italian Ducati motorcycles under licence since 1959. The bikes are adapted for Spanish conditions and the range extends from the 50 cc Mini 2 moped to a 750 GT which develops 60 bhp and has a top speed of 190 km/h. The company also produces a specially modified 350 roadster for police duties and both the 350 and 250 are available in modified form for off-road scrambling.

Head Office: Mototrans, Maquinaria y Elementos De Transporte, S.A., Almogávares, 177–189, Barcelona-5, Spain.

Mototrans   **49.6 cc 50TT Ducati**

Mototrans   **47.6 cc Mini 2 Ducati**

MV Agusta (Italy)

MV Agusta is one of the living legends of the world of motorcycling. Since 1946 the factory at Cascina Costa has produced a steady stream of successful racing bikes which in the hands of riders like Giacomo Agostini and Phil Read, have given the Count Agusta family a tally of over 40 world championships. The factory also makes Bell helicopters and has never really gone in for quantity production of its motorcycles. MV bikes are built to extremely high specifications and their performance and cost tends to limit their sales to a small, somewhat select band of enthusiasts.

Head Office: MV Meccanica Verghera S.p.A., Milano, Viale Adriatico, 50, Italy.

MV Agusta 750S America

Engine:
Type 4-str dohc four
Bore×Stroke 67×56 mm
Capacity 789.7 cc
Compression ratio 9.5:1
Carburettors 4/26 mm Dell'Orto
Maximum power 86 @ 8 500*
Fuel tank 23 l

Transmission:
Gears/Clutch 5/wmp

Electrical:
Ignition 12v/32 Ah/b&c/A
Starting electric
Notes: Shaft drive. Tail section is adjustable for pillion passenger.

Braking:
Front/Rear 280 mm dc/200 mm dm
Front tyres 3.50×18 road
Rear tyres 4.00×18 road

Suspension:
Front/Rear T/SA (3-pos.)

Dimensions:
Ground clearance 165 mm
Seat height 812 mm
Wheelbase 1 390 mm
Overall length 2 110 mm
Dry weight 230 kg

Performance:
Top speed 220 km/h
Fuel consumption 8.1 l/100 km

MV Agusta 350 Sport

Engine:
Type 4-str ohv twin
Bore×Stroke 63×56 mm
Capacity 349 cc
Compression ratio 9.5:1
Carburettors 2/24 mm Dell'Orto
Maximum power 40 @ 8 500*
Fuel tank 19 l

Transmission:
Gears/Clutch 5/wmp

Electrical:
Ignition 12 v/9 Ah/ε/A
Starting kick

Notes:

Braking:
Front/Rear disc/disc
Front tyres 2.75×18 road
Rear tyres 3.25×18 road

Suspension:
Front/Rear T/SA

Dimensions:
Ground clearance ...
Seat height ...
Wheelbase 1 310 mm
Overall length 1 970 mm
Dry weight 160 kg

Performance:
Top speed 170 km/h
Fuel consumption 5.3 l/100 km

MV Agusta 125 Sport

Engine:
Type 4-str ohv single
Bore×Stroke 53×56 mm
Capacity 123.5 cc
Compression ratio 9.5:1
Carburettors 1/22 mm Dell'Orto
Maximum power 14 @ 8 500*
Fuel tank 14 l

Transmission:
Gears/Clutch 5/wmp

Electrical:
Ignition 12 v/6 Ah/ε/A
Starting kick

Notes:

Braking:
Front/Rear disc/drum
Front tyres 2.75×18 road
Rear tyres 4.00×18 road

Suspension:
Front/Rear T/SA

Dimensions:
Ground clearance ...
Seat height ...
Wheelbase 1 300 mm
Overall length 1 980 mm
Dry weight 103 kg

Performance:
Top speed 120 km/h
Fuel consumption 3.1 l/100 km

MZ (East Germany)

The MZ factory was created after the last war from I.F.A. Motorcycles in the original DKW works at Zschopau, south-west of Dresden. MZ is the brand label of the IFA-Kombinat Zweiräder Group which is the nationalized vehicle industry of East Germany. In addition to the road range, MZ produces moto-cross bikes and it has raced 250 cc 2-stroke twins with water-cooling and rotary inlet valves. The 250 ISDT model develops 32 hp and is a replica of the factory bikes which have been so successful in ISDT competition.

Head Office: MZ VEB Motorradwerk Zschopau, DDR – 936 Zschopau.
UK Concessionaires: Wilf Green Ltd, 369/373 Abbeydale Road, Sheffield 7.

MZ TS 250

Engine:
Type 2-str single
Bore × Stroke 69 × 65 mm
Capacity 243 cc
Compression ratio 9.5:1
Carburettors 1/30 mm BVF
Maximum power 21 @ 5 800*
Fuel tank 17.5 l

Transmission:
Gears/Clutch 4/wmp

Electrical:
Ignition 6 v/12 Ah/b&c/D
Starting kick
Notes: TS 150 develops 12.5 bhp.

Braking:
Front/Rear 160 mm drums
Front tyres 3.00 × 16 road
Rear tyres 3.25 × 16 road

Suspension:
Front/Rear T/SA (2-pos.)

Dimensions:
Ground clearance 178 mm
Seat height 762 mm
Wheelbase 1 346 mm
Overall length 2 050 mm
Dry weight 130 kg

Performance:
Top speed 130 km/h
Fuel consumption 4 l/100 km

MZ ES 150/1 Trophy

Engine:
Type 2-str single
Bore×Stroke 56×58 mm
Capacity 143 cc
Compression ratio 10:1
Carburettors 1/24 mm BVF
Maximum power 12.5 @ 6 000
Fuel tank 11.5 l

Transmission:
Gears/Clutch 4/wmp

Electrical:
Ignition 6 v/12 Ah/b&c/D
Starting kick

Notes: 125 model develops 11 bhp.

Braking:
Front/Rear 150 mm drums
Front tyres 2.75×18 road
Rear tyres 3.00×18 road

Suspension:
Front/Rear rocker arm

Dimensions:
Ground clearance 165 mm
Seat height 810 mm
Wheelbase 1 250 mm
Overall length 1 990 mm
Dry weight 105 kg

Performance:
Top speed 105 km/h
Fuel consumption 3 l/100 km

Negrini (Italy)

Cross

Engine:
Type 2-str Morini single
Bore × Stroke 39 × 41.8 mm
Capacity 49 cc
Compression ratio 8.5:1
Carburettors 1/19 mm Dell'Orto
Maximum power 6.5 @ 8 000
Fuel tank 11 l

Transmission:
Gears/Clutch 4/5/wmp

Electrical:
Ignition 6 v/magneto
Starting kick or pedal

Notes:

Braking:
Front/Rear 118 mm drums
Front tyres 2.50 × 19 trials
Rear tyres 3.00 × 17 trials

Suspension:
Front/Rear T/SA

Dimensions:
Ground clearance 180 mm
Seat height 740 mm
Wheelbase 1 170 mm
Overall length 1 730 mm
Dry weight ...

Performance:
Top speed ...
Fuel consumption 1.9 l/100 km

Negrini 5/M Turbo Star

Engine:
Type 2-str Morini single
Bore × Stroke 39 × 41.8 mm
Capacity 49 cc
Compression ratio 8.5:1
Carburettors 1/19 mm Dell'Orto
Maximum power 6.5 @ 4 500
Fuel tank ...

Transmission:
Gears/Clutch 5/wmp

Electrical:
Ignition 6 v/magneto
Starting kick

Notes: Also 4-speed Turbo model

Braking:
Front/Rear 118 mm drums
Front tyres 2.25 × 18 road
Rear tyres 2.25 × 18 road

Suspension:
Front/Rear T/SA

Dimensions:
Ground clearance ...
Seat height 740 mm
Wheelbase 1 170 mm
Overall length 1 730 mm
Dry weight ...

Performance:
Top speed 75 km/h
Fuel consumption 1.9 l/100 km

Negrini Ecole

Engine:
Type 2-str horizontal single
Bore × Stroke 39 × 41.8 mm
Capacity 47.6 cc
Compression ratio 8.5:1
Carburettors 1/12 mm Dell'Orto
Maximum power 1.5 @ 4 500
Fuel tank 4 l

Transmission:
Gears/Clutch single/A

Electrical:
Ignition 6 v/magneto
Starting pedal

Notes:

Braking:
Front/Rear 118 mm drums
Front tyres 2.50 × 16 road
Rear tyres 2.50 × 16 road

Suspension:
Front/Rear T/SA

Dimensions:
Ground clearance ...
Seat height 740 mm
Wheelbase 1 040 mm
Overall length 1 550 mm
Dry weight ...

Performance:
Top speed 50 km/h
Fuel consumption 1.9 l/100 km

Negrini Turismo

Engine:
Type   2-str Morini single
Bore × Stroke   39 × 41.8 mm
Capacity   47.6 cc
Compression ratio   8.5:1
Carburettors   1/12 mm Dell'Orto
Maximum power   1.5 @ 4 500
Fuel tank   4 l

Transmission:
Gears/Clutch   3/wmp

Electrical:
Ignition   6 v/magneto
Starting   pedal

Notes:

Braking:
Front/Rear   118 mm drums
Front tyres   2.25 × 16 road
Rear tyres   2.25 × 16 road

Suspension:
Front/Rear   T/SA

Dimensions:
Ground clearance   180 mm
Seat height   740 mm
Wheelbase   1 040 mm
Overall length   1 550 mm
Dry weight   ...

Performance:
Top speed   50 km/h
Fuel consumption   1.2 l/100 km

The family firm of Negrini was founded in 1934 and now manufactures motorcycles, mopeds, three-wheelers and folding bicycles. The large moped range of 15 models includes mini bikes such as the Gipsy and lively 5-speeders like the Cross Fuoristrada. Negrini also assembles 4-speed 2-stroke motorcycles with 100 and 125 cc Morini engines.
Head Office: Fabbrica Ciclomotori di Mauro Negrini, 41056 Savignano Sul Panaro (Modena), Via Claudia, 847, Italy.
UK Concessionaires: Slater Bros., Collington, Bromyard, Herefordshire.

Norton Villiers Triumph (UK)

The history of the formation of NVT is a complicated picture of amalgamations which tell the story of the decline of British motorcycle manufacture. Generations of enthusiasts who have ridden Aerial Square Fours, 'Cammy Ajays', 'Beezer Goldies', Francis-Barnett and James 2-strokes, Matchless Vee-twins, Norton Big Fours and Triumph Speed Twins must be saddened to see these great names from British motorcycle engineering represented now by an odd mixture of aging superbikes, prototype 2-strokes and small mopeds fitted with imported engines and other components.

Norton and Triumph trace their ancestry back to the first developments of motorcycles and both can claim many sporting successes, Norton being linked especially with the TT races which it dominated during the 1930s and Triumph with world speed records in the fifties. Both companies have always produced riders' machines offering strong construction, outstanding road holding and exceptional performance. Technically, Norton introduced the famous 'featherbed' frame which set the standards for post-war frame design, and recently it tackled the problem of vibration in big bikes with its Isolastic system (see page 12). A highly innovatory Triumph design was the transverse vertical twin of 1937 which was widely copied by the world's manufacturers.

In 1956 Norton was bought by Associated Motor Cycles Ltd which subsequently went into liquidation in 1966. Manganese Bronze bought the Norton name with various other assets and developed Norton Villiers as a going concern. The financial difficulties of the BSA/Triumph group in 1971/72 led to the absorption of its motorcycle activities by Norton Villiers at the instigation of the Government in March 1973. The decision to close the Triumph Meriden factory precipitated the 18-month workers' sit-in which was finally resolved in the form of a government-sponsored co-operative despite NVT's claim that a three-factory set-up was not viable without the help of substantial government-backing. The publication of the Boston Consulting Group's analysis of British motorcycle manufacture in the summer of 1975 identified several costly rescue operations for the ailing industry but the Government felt unable to continue financial support. At the end of August NVT began a substantial run-down which resulted first in the closure of the Norton factory at Wolverhampton followed by the final winding-up of NVT Manufacturing at Small Heath in December.

By the end of 1975 the UK's last major motorcycle manufacturer was in fragments. A new company — NVT Motorcycle Ltd — had been formed to take over the world-wide distribution functions and development work of Norton Triumph International. Production of the NVT range, including the Interpol used by some 50 police forces around the world, had ceased and a new, small company, NVT Engineering, had been formed with government aid to ensure continued provision of Norton and Triumph spares. The Meriden Co-operative was continuing production of Bonneville 750 Twins and seeking independence of NVT by outright purchase of the Triumph name and patents. At the closed Wolverhampton plant and workers' action committee was hopeful of attracting private investment to produce the Norton Commando, a new, stepped-piston 2-stroke twin and an Italian-engined 2-stroke moped.

NVT Motorcycles Ltd, Lynn Lane, Sherstone, Staffordshire, England.
NVT Engineering, Montgomery Street, Birmingham, England.
Triumph Co-operative: Meriden Works, Allesley, Coventry, England.

NVT

Engine:
Type 4-str ohv twin
Bore × Stroke   77 × 89 mm
Capacity   828 cc
Compression ratio   8.5:1
Carburettors   2/27 mm Amal
Maximum power   58 @ 5 900
Fuel tank   11 l

Transmission:
Gears/Clutch   4/wmp

Electrical:
Ignition   12 v/15 Ah/b&c/A
Starting   electric

Notes: Also available as Interstate (24 l tank), Interpol and Norton Club Racer.

NVT

Engine:
Type 4-str ohv triple
Bore × Stroke   67 × 70 mm
Capacity   740 cc
Compression ratio   9.5:1
Carburettors   3/27 mm Amal
Maximum power   58 @ 7 250
Fuel tank   17 l

Transmission:
Gears/Clutch   5/dsp

Electrical:
Ignition   12 v/15 Ah/b&c/A
Starting   electric

Notes:

NVT

Engine:
Type 4-str ohv twin
Bore × Stroke   76 × 82 mm
Capacity   744 cc
Compression ratio   7.9:1
Carburettors   2/30 mm Amal
Maximum power   52 @ 6 500
Fuel tank   18 l

Transmission:
Gears/Clutch   5/wmp

Electrical:
Ignition   12 v/12 Ah/b&c/A
Starting   kick

Notes:

Commando Mk 3 Roadster

Braking:
Front/Rear   270 mm discs
Front tyres   4.10 × 19 road
Rear tyres   4.10 × 19 road

Suspension:
Front/Rear   T/SA (2-pos.)

Dimensions:
Ground clearance   150 mm
Seat height   815 mm
Wheelbase   1 450 mm
Overall length   2 230 mm
Dry weight   212 kg

Performance:
Top speed   190 km/h (p)
Fuel consumption 6.5 l/100 km (p)

Trident T160

Braking:
Front/Rear   254 mm discs
Front tyres   4.10 × 19 road
Rear tyres   4.10 × 19 road

Suspension:
Front/Rear   T/SA (2-pos.)

Dimensions:
Ground clearance   160 mm
Seat height   790 mm
Wheelbase   1 470 mm
Overall length   2 230 mm
Dry weight   227 kg

Performance:
Top speed   190 km/h (p)
Fuel consumption 5.8 l/100 km (p)

Meriden Bonneville 750

Braking:
Front/Rear   254 mm discs
Front tyres   3.25 × 19 road
Rear tyres   4.00 × 18 road

Suspension:
Front/Rear   T/SA (2-pos.)

Dimensions:
Ground clearance   180 mm
Seat height   790 mm
Wheelbase   1 420 mm
Overall length   2 220 mm
Dry weight   181 kg

Performance:
Top speed   185 km/h (p)
Fuel consumption   6.0 l/100 km (p)

Ossa (Spain)

Engine:
Type 2-str single
Bore×Stroke 65×77 mm
Capacity 350 cc
Compression ratio 11.5:1
Carburettors 1/27 mm Amal
Maximum power ...
Fuel tank 6 l

Transmission:
Gears/Clutch 5/wmp

Electrical:
Ignition 6 v/ε/magneto
Starting kick

Notes: Fitted with auxiliary silencer for road use.

Ossa

Engine:
Type 2-str single
Bore×Stroke 60×72 mm
Capacity 244 cc
Compression ratio 11.5:1
Carburettors 1/27 mm Amal
Maximum power 17 @ 6 500
Fuel tank 8 l

Transmission:
Gears/Clutch 5/wmp

Electrical:
Ignition 6 v/8 Ah/ε/magneto
Starting kick

Notes: 250 Explorer model has similar specification.

Ossa

Engine:
Type 2-str single
Bore×Stroke 60×72 mm
Capacity 244 cc
Compression ratio 11.5:1
Carburettors 1/32 mm/Amal
Maximum power 28 @ 6 800
Fuel tank 13 l

Transmission:
Gears/Clutch 5/wmp

Electrical:
Ignition 6 v/8 Ah/ε/magneto
Starting kick

Notes:

Trial 350 M.A.R.

Braking:
Front/Rear 122 mm drums
Front tyres 2.75×21 trials
Rear tyres 4.00×18 trials

Suspension:
Front/Rear T/SA (3-pos.)

Dimensions:
Ground clearance 250 mm
Seat height 860 mm
Wheelbase 1 320 mm
Overall length ...
Dry weight 87 kg

Performance:
Top speed ...
Fuel consumption ...

250 Trial M.A.R.

Braking:
Front/Rear 122 mm drums
Front tyres 3.00×21 trials
Rear tyres 4.00×18 trials

Suspension:
Front/Rear T/SA (3-pos.)

Dimensions:
Ground clearance 250 mm
Seat height 830 mm
Wheelbase 1 290 mm
Overall length 2 030 mm
Dry weight 88 kg

Performance:
Top speed 120 km/h
Fuel consumption ...

250 Super Pioneer

Braking:
Front/Rear 122 mm dm/150 mm dm
Front tyres 3.00×21 trials
Rear tyres 4.50×18 trials

Suspension:
Front/Rear T/SA (3-pos.)

Dimensions:
Ground clearance 270 mm
Seat height 860 mm
Wheelbase 1 392 mm
Overall length 2 080 mm
Dry weight 93 kg

Performance:
Top speed 130 km/h
Fuel consumption ...

Ossa — Enduro 125

Engine:
Type 2-stroke single
Bore × Stroke 54 × 54 mm
Capacity 125 cc
Compression ratio 11.5:1
Carburettors 1/30 mm Amal
Maximum power 21 @ 7 000
Fuel tank 9 l

Transmission:
Gears/Clutch 5/wmp

Electrical:
Ignition 6 v/ε/magneto
Starting kick

Notes:

Braking:
Front/Rear 122 mm dm/150 mm dm
Front tyres 3.00 × 21 trials
Rear tyres 4.00 × 18 trials

Suspension:
Front/Rear T/SA (3-pos.)

Dimensions:
Ground clearance 270 mm
Seat height 860 mm
Wheelbase 1 383 mm
Overall length 2 080 mm
Dry weight 93 kg

Performance:
Top speed 115 km/h
Fuel consumption ...

Ossa, Bultaco and Montesa form the big three in Spain's motorcycle industry. Ossa began motorcycle production in 1946 but before that the firm had been long-established in the manufacture of projector equipment for cinemas. Ossa specializes in enduro and off-road machines which are fitted with powerful engines in lightweight frames to achieve sensitive and sure handling. In the hands of riders like Mick Andrews Ossa bikes have won many international trials competitions and they have been very successful in the United States market where off-road motorcycle sport is extremely popular. The Ossa factory is a modern one and most components are cast and machined there – only suspension units, wheels and electrical parts being bought in. Ossa was one of the early pioneers in the use of CDI ignition on its models.

Head Office: Maquinaria Cinematografica, S.A., Poligona Industrial Zona Franca Sector B – Calle B, Barcelona-4, Spain.
UK Concessionaires: Ossa Moto (UK) Ltd, Ferndown Industrial Estate, Ferndown, Dorset.

Peugeot (France)

Peugeot was one of the earliest pioneers in the manufacture of motorcycles. Bicycles were being made as early as 1882, and under the trade name of Les Fils de Peugeot Frères' manufacture of motorcycles and cars began in 1890. In 1926 a separate company, Cycles Peugeot, was started to concentrate on motorcycles, and its 500 cc vertical twins achieved considerable racing success. In the mid-fifties Peugeot stopped making motorcycles and concentrated on mopeds. Peugeot offers over 25 basic models and both bicycles and mopeds are made under licence in 14 countries. The company also makes parts for carts, elevating loading platforms and storage containers.

Head Office: Cycles Peugeot, 251 Boulevard Peraire, 75 852 Paris, France.
UK Concessionaires: Cycles Peugeot (UK), Edison Road, Bedford MK41 0HU.

Peugeot   **TSN**

Engine:
Type 2-str single
Bore × Stroke 40 × 39 mm
Capacity 49 cc
Compression ratio 7.4:1
Carburettors 1/14 mm Gurtner
Maximum power 2 @ 5500
Fuel tank 10 l

Transmission:
Gears/Clutch 3/wmp

Electrical:
Ignition 6 v/magneto
Starting pedal

Notes: SPN model has clip-ons.

Braking:
Front/Rear 90 mm dm/100 mm dm
Front tyres 2.25 × 17 road
Rear tyres 2.75 × 17 road

Suspension:
Front/Rear T/SA

Dimensions:
Ground clearance ...
Seat height ...
Wheelbase ...
Overall length ...
Dry weight 56 kg

Performance:
Top speed 45 km/h
Fuel consumption 2 l/100 km

Peugeot

GT 10 F3

Engine:
Type   2-str single
Bore×Stroke   40×39 mm
Capacity   49 cc
Compression ratio   7.4:1
Carburettors   1/12 mm Gurtner
Maximum power   2 @ 5 500
Fuel tank   3.7 l

Transmission:
Gears/Clutch   3/wmp

Electrical:
Ignition   6 v/magneto
Starting   pedal

Notes:

Braking:
Front/Rear   80 mm drums
Front tyres   3.00×10 road
Rear tyres   3.00×10 road

Suspension:
Front/Rear   T/SA

Dimensions:
Ground clearance   ...
Seat height   ...
Wheelbase   ...
Overall length   ...
Dry weight   56 km

Performance:
Top speed   45 km/h
Fuel consumption   2 l/100 km

Peugeot

TSA

Engine:
Type   2-str single
Bore×Stroke   40×39 mm
Capacity   49 cc
Compression ratio   8.4:1
Carburettors   1/12 mm Gurtner
Maximum power   1.9 @ 5 500
Fuel tank   7.5 l

Transmission:
Gears/Clutch   variable/A

Electrical:
Ignition   6 v/magneto
Starting   pedal

Notes:

Braking:
Front/Rear   80 mm drums
Front tyres   2.25×17 road
Rear tyres   2.25×17 road

Suspension:
Front/Rear   T/SA

Dimensions:
Ground clearance   ...
Seat height   ...
Wheelbase   ...
Overall length   ...
Dry weight   49 kg

Performance:
Top speed   45 km/h
Fuel consumption   2 l/100 km

Peugeot

104N

Engine:
Type   2-str single
Bore×Stroke   40×39 mm
Capacity   49 cc
Compression ratio   8.4:1
Carburettors   1/12 mm Gurtner
Maximum power   1.9 @ 5 500
Fuel tank   3.7 l

Transmission:
Gears/Clutch   single/A

Electrical:
Ignition   6 v/magneto
Starting   pedal

Notes:

Braking:
Front/Rear   80 mm drums
Front tyres   2.25×15 road
Rear tyres   2.25×15 road

Suspension:
Front/Rear   T/SA

Dimensions:
Ground clearance   ...
Seat height   ...
Wheelbase   ...
Overall length   ...
Dry weight   43 kg

Performance:
Top speed   45 km/h
Fuel consumption   1.8 l/100 km

Peugeot 103VSC

Engine:
Type 2-str single
Bore×Stroke 40×39 mm
Capacity 49 cc
Compression ratio 8.4:1
Carburettors 1/12 mm Gurtner
Maximum power 1.9 @ 5500
Fuel tank 4 l

Transmission:
Gears/Clutch variable/A

Electrical:
Ignition 6 v/magneto
Starting pedal

Notes: Other models 103, 103V, 103LV, 103LVS.

Braking:
Front/Rear 80 mm drums
Front tyres 2.25×17 road
Rear tyres 2.25×17 road

Suspension:
Front/Rear T/SA

Dimensions:
Ground clearance ...
Seat height ...
Wheelbase ...
Overall length ...
Dry weight 43 kg

Performance:
Top speed 45 km/h
Fuel consumption 2 l/100 km

Peugeot 102KT

Engine:
Type 2-str single
Bore×Stroke 40×39 mm
Capacity 49 cc
Compression ratio 7.4:1
Carburettors 1/12 mm Gurtner
Maximum power 1.5 @ 5000
Fuel tank 3.3 l

Transmission:
Gears/Clutch single/A

Electrical:
Ignition 6 v/magneto
Starting pedal

Notes: Other models 102NMR, 102T and 102R.

Braking:
Front/Rear 70 mm drums
Front tyres 2.00×17 road
Rear tyres 2.00×17 road

Suspension:
Front/Rear T/rigid

Dimensions:
Ground clearance ...
Seat height ...
Wheelbase ...
Overall length ...
Dry weight 35 kg

Performance:
Top speed 45 km/h
Fuel consumption 1.8 l/100 km

Peugeot 101MT

Engine:
Type 2-str single
Bore×Stroke 40×39 mm
Capacity 49 cc
Compression ratio 7.4:1
Carburettors 1/10 mm Gurtner
Maximum power 1 @ 4000
Fuel tank 3 l

Transmission:
Gears/Clutch single/A

Electrical:
Ignition 6 v/magneto
Starting pedal

Notes: Other models 101MR, 101T and 101S.

Braking:
Front/Rear 70 mm drums
Front tyres 2.00×16 road
Rear tyres 2.00×16 road

Suspension:
Front/Rear T/rigid

Dimensions:
Ground clearance ...
Seat height ...
Wheelbase ...
Overall length ...
Dry weight 32 kg

Performance:
Top speed 35 km/h
Fuel consumption 1.6 l/100 km

Puch (Austria)

Engine:
Type 2-str single
Bore × Stroke 38 × 43 mm
Capacity 48.8 cc
Compression ratio 11:1
Carburettors 1/17 mm Bing
Maximum power 5 @ 8500
Fuel tank 6.5 l

Transmission:
Gears/Clutch 4/wmp

Electrical:
Ignition 6 v/4.5 Ah/magneto
Starting kick/pedal

Notes: GP Special version fitted with 185 mm front disc.

Puch

Engine:
Type 2-str single
Bore × Stroke 40 × 39.7 mm
Capacity 49 cc
Compression ratio 12:1
Carburettors 1/20 mm Bing
Maximum power 7 @ 8500
Fuel tank 7.6 l

Transmission:
Gears/Clutch 6/wmp

Electrical:
Ignition 6 v/4.5 Ah/ε/magneto
Starting kick

Notes:

Puch

Engine:
Type 2-str single
Bore × Stroke 38 × 43 mm
Capacity 48.8 cc
Compression ratio 11:1
Carburettors 1/17 mm Bing
Maximum power 2.6 @ 5500
Fuel tank 10 l

Transmission:
Gears/Clutch 4/wmp

Electrical:
Ignition 6 v/magneto
Starting kick

Notes:

M50 Grand Prix

Braking:
Front/Rear 114 mm drums
Front tyres 2.75 × 21
Rear tyres 2.75 × 21

Suspension:
Front/Rear T/SA

Dimensions:
Ground clearance 190 mm
Seat height 770 mm
Wheelbase 1 205 mm
Overall length 1 830 mm
Dry weight 74 kg

Performance:
Top speed 75 km/h
Fuel consumption 3 l/100 km

M50 Jet

Braking:
Front/Rear 140 mm drums
Front tyres 2.50 × 17 road
Rear tyres 3.00 × 17 road

Suspension:
Front/Rear T/SA

Dimensions:
Ground clearance 160 mm
Seat height 800 mm
Wheelbase 1 240 mm
Overall length 1 900 mm
Dry weight 92 kg

Performance:
Top speed 85 km/h
Fuel consumption 3 l/100 km

M50 Cross

Braking:
Front/Rear 140 mm drums
Front tyres 2.50 × 23 road
Rear tyres 3.00 × 18 road

Suspension:
Front/Rear T/SA

Dimensions:
Ground clearance 190 mm
Seat height 790 mm
Wheelbase 1 250 mm
Overall length 1 950 mm
Dry weight 84 kg

Performance:
Top speed 40 km/h
Fuel consumption 1.8 l/100 km

Puch

VZ50

Engine:
Type   2-str single
Bore × Stroke   38 × 43 mm
Capacity   49 cc
Compression ratio   11:1
Carburettors   1/12 mm Bing
Maximum power   3.25 @ 6 000
Fuel tank   10.5 l

Transmission:
Gears/Clutch   3/wmp

Electrical:
Ignition   6 v/magneto
Starting   pedal

Notes:

Braking:
Front/Rear   105 mm drums
Front tyres   2.75 × 21 road
Rear tyres   2.75 × 21 road

Suspension:
Front/Rear   T/SA

Dimensions:
Ground clearance   140 mm
Seat height   800 mm
Wheelbase   1 200 mm
Overall length   1 830 mm
Dry weight   55 kg

Performance:
Top speed   60 km/h
Fuel consumption   2 l/100 km

Puch

DS 50L

Engine:
Type   2-str single
Bore × Stroke   38 × 43 mm
Capacity   48.8 cc
Compression ratio   11:1
Carburettors   1/14 mm Bing
Maximum power   2.6 @ 5 000
Fuel tank   10.5 l

Transmission:
Gears/Clutch   4/wmp

Electrical:
Ignition   6 v/magneto
Starting   kick

Notes:

Braking:
Front/Rear   105 mm drums
Front tyres   3.00 × 12 road
Rear tyres   3.00 × 12 road

Suspension:
Front/Rear   T/SA

Dimensions:
Ground clearance   125 mm
Seat height   780 mm
Wheelbase   1 150 mm
Overall length   1 680 mm
Dry weight   74 kg

Performance:
Top speed   40 km/h
Fuel consumption   1.8 l/100 km

Puch

Mini Dakota

Engine:
Type   2-str single
Bore × Stroke   38 × 43 mm
Capacity   48.8 cc
Compression   11.5:1
Carburettors   1/17 mm Bing
Maximum power   4.9 @ 6 600
Fuel tank   8 l

Transmission:
Gears/Clutch   4/wmp

Electrical:
Ignition   6 v/magneto
Starting   kick

Notes: Made in Spain by Avello S.A.

Braking:
Front/Rear   110 mm drums
Front tyres   2.50 × 18 trials
Rear tyres   2.50 × 17 trials

Suspension:
Front/Rear   T/SA

Dimensions:
Ground clearance   220 mm
Seat height   720 mm
Wheelbase   1 170 mm
Overall length   1 770 mm
Dry weight   61 kg

Performance:
Top speed   70 km/h
Fuel consumption   3 l/100 km

Puch   **Maxi S2**

Engine:
Type 2-str single
Bore × Stroke 38 × 43 mm
Capacity 48.8 cc
Compression ratio 10.5:1
Carburettors 1/12 mm Bing
Maximum power 2.2 @ 4 500
Fuel tank 3.2 l

Transmission:
Gears/Clutch 2/wmp

Electrical:
Ignition 6 v/magneto
Starting pedal

Notes: Maxi D has dual seat. Maxi N has rigid rear suspension. Maxi S has single speed.

Braking:
Front/Rear 80 mm dm/90 mm dm
Front tyres 2.00 × 21 road
Rear tyres 2.00 × 21 road

Suspension:
Front/Rear T/SA

Dimensions:
Ground clearance 100 mm
Seat height 770 mm
Wheelbase 1 120 mm
Overall length 1 700 mm
Dry weight 44 kg

Performance:
Top speed 45 km/h
Fuel consumption 1.6 l/100 km

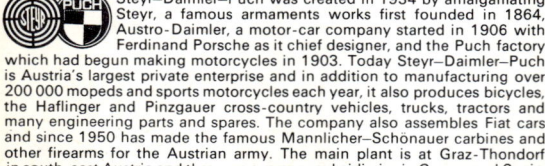

Steyr–Daimler–Puch was created in 1934 by amalgamating Steyr, a famous armaments works first founded in 1864, Austro-Daimler, a motor-car company started in 1906 with Ferdinand Porsche as it chief designer, and the Puch factory which had begun making motorcycles in 1903. Today Steyr–Daimler–Puch is Austria's largest private enterprise and in addition to manufacturing over 200 000 mopeds and sports motorcycles each year, it also produces bicycles, the Haflinger and Pinzgauer cross-country vehicles, trucks, tractors and many engineering parts and spares. The company also assembles Fiat cars and since 1950 has made the famous Mannlicher–Schönauer carbines and other firearms for the Austrian army. The main plant is at Graz-Thondorf in south-east Austria and there are overseas subsidiaries in Greece and Spain.
Head Office: Steyr–Daimler–Puch A.G., Werke Graz, Postf. 423, A-8011 Graz, Austria.
UK Concessionaires: Steyr–Daimler–Puch (Great Britain) Ltd, 211 Lower Parliament Street, Nottingham NG1 1FZ.

Sanglas (Spain) 400E

Engine:
Type 4-str ohv single
Bore × Stroke 82.5 × 79 mm
Capacity 423 cc
Compression ratio 8:1
Carburettors 1/30 mm Amal
Maximum power 30 @ 6 500
Fuel tank 15 l

Transmission:
Gears/Clutch 4/wmp

Electrical:
Ignition 12 v/38 Ah/b&c/D
Starting electric

Notes:

Braking:
Front/Rear 180 mm drums
Front tyres 3.25 × 18 road
Rear tyres 3.25 × 18 road

Suspension:
Front/Rear T/SA (5-pos.)

Dimensions:
Ground clearance 160 mm
Seat height 790 mm
Wheelbase ...
Overall length 2 120 mm
Dry weight 168 kg

Performance'
Top speed 160 km/h
Fuel consumption ...

Unlike other Spanish firms who mainly concentrate on lightweight, sporting 2-strokes, Sanglas has produced, since the early fifties, a series of medium-sized 4-strokes featuring the best of the current technical innovations. The present range includes a 500 cc ohc 4-stroke with electric start, and the 400 model is also available in a police duties version.
Head Office: Sanglas, S.A., Rambla Justo Oliveras, s/n. Hospitalet–Barcelona, Spain.

Silk (UK) 700S

Engine:
Type   2-str twin
Bore × Stroke   76 × 72 mm
Capacity   653 cc
Compression ratio   …
Carburettors   1/32 mm Amal
Maximum power   …
Fuel tank   18 l

Transmission:
Gears/Clutch   4/wmp

Electrical:
Ignition   12 v/ε/A
Starting   kick

Notes: Specification subject to change as development continues.

Braking:
Front/Rear   254 mm dc/178 mm dm
Front tyres   3.60 × 18 road
Rear tyres   4.10 × 18 road

Suspension:
Front/Rear   T/SA

Dimensions:
Ground clearance   200 mm
Seat height   710 mm
Wheelbase   1 420 mm
Overall length   2 060 mm
Dry weight   145 kg

Performance:
Top speed   185 km/h
Fuel consumption   7 l/100 km

The Silk 700S is a limited-production road machine which can be tailor-made to the customer's own specification. Silk Engineering was set up by George Silk and Maurice Patey, and has developed from overhauling and tuning vintage motorcycles to the production of an exclusive all-British motorcycle.

The 700S has a scientifically researched and developed water-cooled, all-aluminium 2-stroke engine which uses a new, patented 'Velocity Contoured' charge/scavenge system that is claimed to give abundant low-speed torque and good fuel consumption. The lightweight duplex frame and small, compact engine design give good handling and road holding. A high quality specification is used for all component parts and includes throttle-controlled lubrication, transistorized ignition and the use of stainless steel for wheel spokes and all nuts and bolts. An annual production of 100 machines is planned.

Head Office: Silk Engineering (Derby) Ltd, Boars Head Mill, Darley Abbey, Derby, England.

SIS (Portugal) — Brasa

Engine:
Type 2-str horizontal single
Bore × Stroke 38 × 42 mm
Capacity 47 cc
Compression ratio ...
Carburettors ...
Maximum power 2.4 h.p.
Fuel tank 6 l

Transmission:
Gears/Clutch single/A

Electrical:
Ignition 6 v/magneto
Starting pedal

Notes:

Front/Rear 100 mm drums
Front tyres 2.25 × 20 road
Rear tyres 2.25 × 20 road

Suspension:
Front/Rear T/SA

Dimensions:
Ground clearance ...
Seat height 790 mm
Wheelbase 1 085 mm
Overall length 1 680 mm
Dry weight 46 kg

Performance:
Top speed 40 km/h
Fuel consumption 1.5 l/100 km

The SIS range of mopeds and lightweight motorcycles is manufactured in a modern factory at Anadia midway between Lisbon and Porto in Portugal. SIS are associated with Fichtel & Sachs AG of Germany and use their 50 series engines in all their models. The rest of the range includes the Minor GT, the Andorinha, the Eko 70 and a lightweight motorcycle, the Felino which features double telescopic shock absorbers at the rear. SIS also manufactures three-wheel pickup trucks.

Head Office: SIS – Veiculos Motorizados, LDA, Apartado 6 – Anadia, Portugal.

SIS

Almirante 5

Engine:
Type 2-str. single
Bore × Stroke 38 × 44 mm
Capacity 49 cc
Compression ratio ...
Carburettors ...
Maximum power 5.3 h.p.
Fuel tank 12 l

Transmission:
Gears/Clutch 5/wmp

Electrical:
Ignition 6 v/magneto
Starting kick

Notes: Also available in 4-speed, fan-cooled engine form.

Braking:
Front/Rear 150 mm drums
Front tyres 2.75 × 21 road
Rear tyres 2.75 × 21 road

Suspension:
Front/Rear T/SA

Dimensions:
Ground clearance 190 mm
Seat height 740 mm
Wheelbase 1 190 mm
Overall length 1 850 mm
Dry weight 76 kg

Performance:
Top speed 75 km/h
Fuel consumption 2 l/100 km

SIS

V5

Engine:
Type 2-str single
Bore × Stroke 38 × 44 mm
Capacity 49 cc
Compression ratio ...
Carburettors ...
Maximum power 5.3 h.p.
Fuel tank 16 l

Transmission:
Gears/Clutch 5/wmp

Electrical:
Ignition 6 v/magneto
Starting kick

Notes: Also available with 6.5 hp Sachs 50SA.

Braking:
Front/Rear 115 mm drums
Front tyres 2.75 × 21 road
Rear tyres 2.75 × 21 road

Suspension:
Front/Rear T/SA

Dimensions:
Ground clearance 180 mm
Seat height 730 mm
Wheelbase 1 200 mm
Overall length 1 800 mm
Dry weight 68 kg

Performance:
Top speed 75 km/h
Fuel consumption 2 l/100 km

SIS

Lebre

Engine:
Type 2-str fan-cooled single
Bore × Stroke 38 × 42 mm
Capacity 47 cc
Compression ratio ...
Carburettors ...
Maximum power 4.3 h.p.
Fuel tank 12 l

Transmission:
Gears/Clutch 4/wmp

Electrical:
Ignition 6 v/magneto
Starting kick

Notes:

Braking:
Front/Rear 115 mm drums
Front tyres 2.75 × 21 road
Rear tyres 2.75 × 21 road

Suspension:
Front/Rear T/SA

Dimensions:
Ground clearance 180 mm
Seat height 740 mm
Wheelbase 1 100 mm
Overall length 1 770 mm
Dry weight 67 kg

Performance:
Top speed 70 km/h
Fuel consumption 2 l/100 km

Suzuki (Japan)

RE-5

Engine:
Type   NSU/Wankel rotary
Bore × Stroke   single chamber
Capacity   497 cc
Compression ratio   9.4:1
Carburettors   1/32 mm Mikuni†
Maximum power   62 @ 6 500*
Fuel tank   17 l

Transmission:
Gears/Clutch   5/wmp

Electrical:
Ignition   12 v/24 Ah/CDI/A
Starting   electric

Notes: †Twin choke, two stage carburettor (18/32).

Braking:
Front/Rear   300 mm dc/178 mm dm
Front tyres   3.25×19 road
Rear tyres   4.00×18 road

Suspension:
Front/Rear   T/SA (5-pos.)

Dimensions:
Ground clearance   170 mm
Seat height   813 mm
Wheelbase   1 500 mm
Overall length   2 220 mm
Dry weight   230 kg

Performance:
Top speed   184 km/h (p)
Fuel consumption   8 l/100 km (p)

Suzuki

GT 750A

Engine:
Type   2-str triple
Bore × Stroke   70×64 mm
Capacity   738 cc
Compression ratio   6.9:1
Carburettors   3/40 mm Mikuni
Maximum power   70 @ 6 500
Fuel tank   17 l

Transmission:
Gears/Clutch   5/wmp

Electrical:
Ignition   12 v/14 Ah/b&c/A
Starting   electric

Notes: Water-cooled engine.

Braking:
Front/Rear   273 mm dc/200 mm dm
Front tyres   3.25×19 road
Rear tyres   4.00×18 road

Suspension:
Front/Rear   T/SA (5-pos.)

Dimensions:
Ground clearance   140 mm
Seat height   813 mm
Wheelbase   1 470 mm
Overall length   2 215 mm
Dry weight   230 kg

Performance:
Top speed   200 km/h (p)
Fuel consumption   6.4 l/100 km (p)

Suzuki

GT 500A

Engine:
Type   2-str twin
Bore × Stroke   70×64 mm
Capacity   492 cc
Compression ratio   6.6:1
Carburettors   2/32 mm Mikuni
Maximum power   44 @ 6 000
Fuel tank   16 l

Transmission:
Gears/Clutch   5/wmp

Electrical:
Ignition   12 v/7 Ah/ε/A
Starting   kick

Notes:

Braking:
Front/Rear   270 mm dc/178 mm dm
Front tyres   3.25×19 road
Rear tyres   4.00×18 road

Suspension:
Front/Rear   T/SA (5-pos.)

Dimensions:
Ground clearance   160 mm
Seat height   787 mm
Wheelbase   1 448 mm
Overall length   2 195 mm
Dry weight   187 kg

Performance:
Top speed   176 km/h (p)
Fuel consumption   6.3 l/100 km (p)

Suzuki

Engine:
Type 2-str triple
Bore × Stroke 54 × 54 mm
Capacity 317 cc
Compression ratio 7.2:1
Carburettors 3/24 mm Mikuni
Maximum power 37 @ 7 500
Fuel tank 15 l

Transmission:
Gears/Clutch 6/wmp

Electrical:
Ignition 12 v/b&c/A
Starting kick

Notes:

380 GTM

Braking:
Front/Rear 270 mm dc/180 mm dm
Front tyres 3.00 × 19 road
Rear tyres 3.50 × 18 road

Suspension:
Front/Rear T/SA (5-pos.)

Dimensions:
Ground clearance 145 mm
Seat height 730 mm
Wheelbase 1 380 mm
Overall length 2 090 mm
Dry weight 171 kg

Performance:
Top speed 176 km/h (p)
Fuel consumption 6 l/100 km (p)

Suzuki

Engine:
Type 2-str twin
Bore × Stroke 54 × 54 mm
Capacity 247 cc
Compression ratio 7.5:1
Carburettors 2/28 mm Mikuni
Maximum power 33 @ 7 000
Fuel tank 15 l

Transmission:
Gears/Clutch 6/wmp

Electrical:
Ignition 12 v/7 Ah/b&c/A
Starting kick

Notes:

GT 250A

Braking:
Front/Rear 270 mm dc/180 mm dm
Front tyres 3.00 × 18 road
Rear tyres 3.25 × 18 road

Suspension:
Front/Rear T/SA (5-pos.)

Dimensions:
Ground clearance 160 mm
Seat height 800 mm
Wheelbase 1 310 mm
Overall length 2 045 mm
Dry weight 146 kg

Performance:
Top speed 152 km/h (p)
Fuel consumption 5.6 l/100 km (p)

Suzuki

Engine:
Type 2-str reed-valve single
Bore × Stroke 70 × 64 mm
Capacity 246 cc
Compression ratio 6.7:1
Carburettors 1/28 mm Mikuni
Maximum power 23 @ 6 500
Fuel tank 9 l

Transmission:
Gears/Clutch 5/wmp

Electrical:
Ignition 6 v/ε/magneto
Starting kick

Notes: TS 400, TS 185, TS 100 and TS 50 also available.

TS 250A

Braking:
Front/Rear 107 mm drums
Front tyres 3.00 × 21 trials
Rear tyres 4.00 × 18 trials

Suspension:
Front/Rear T/SA (5-pos.)

Dimensions:
Ground clearance 250 mm
Seat height 730 mm
Wheelbase 1 415 mm
Overall length 2 210 mm
Dry weight 111 kg

Performance:
Top speed 125 km/h (p)
Fuel consumption …

Suzuki

TS 125A

Engine:
Type 2-str single
Bore×Stroke 56×50 mm
Capacity 123 cc
Compression ratio 6.7:1
Carburettors 1/24 mm Mikuni
Maximum power 14 @ 7 000
Fuel tank 7 l

Transmission:
Gears/Clutch 5/wmp

Electrical:
Ignition 6 v/4 Ah/magneto
Starting kick

Notes: TC model has 4-speeds. TC variants include TC 100 and TC 185.

Braking:
Front/Rear 160 mm drums
Front tyres 2.75×21 trials
Rear tyres 3.25×18 trials

Suspension:
Front/Rear T/SA (5-pos.)

Dimensions:
Ground clearance 235 mm
Seat height 750 mm
Wheelbase 1 310 mm
Overall length 2 050 mm
Dry weight 90 kg

Performance:
Top speed 105 km/h (p)
Fuel consumption 4.6 l/100 km (p)

Suzuki

B120 Student

Engine:
Type 2-str single
Bore×Stroke 52×56 mm
Capacity 118 cc
Compression ratio 6.7:1
Carburettors 1/20 mm Mikuni
Maximum power 9.8 @ 7 000
Fuel tank 8 l

Transmission:
Gears/Clutch 4/wmp

Electrical:
Ignition 6 v/4 Ah/magneto
Starting kick

Notes: Fitted with fully enclosed chain.

Braking:
Front/Rear 115 mm drums
Front tyres 2.50×17 road
Rear tyres 2.50×17 road

Suspension:
Front/Rear T/SA (3-pos.)

Dimensions:
Ground clearance 152 mm
Seat height 762 mm
Wheelbase 1 120 mm
Overall length 1 905 mm
Dry weight 85 kg

Performance:
Top speed 110 km/h (p)
Fuel consumption 3 l/100 km (p)

Suzuki

A100

Engine:
Type 2-str rotary-valve single
Bore×Stroke 50×50 mm
Capacity 98 cc
Compression ratio 6.5:1
Carburettors 1/20 mm Mikuni
Maximum power 9.3 @ 7 500
Fuel tank 7 l

Transmission:
Gears/Clutch 4/wmp

Electrical:
Ignition 6 v/magneto
Starting kick

Notes:

Braking:
Front/Rear 140 mm drums
Front tyres 2.50×18 road
Rear tyres 2.50×18 road

Suspension:
Front/Rear T/SA

Dimensions:
Ground clearance 135 mm
Seat height 850 mm
Wheelbase 1 200 mm
Overall length 1 830 mm
Dry weight 83 kg

Performance:
Top speed 110 km/h (p)
Fuel consumption …

Suzuki RV 125

Engine:
Type 2-str single
Bore×Stroke 56×50 mm
Capacity 123 cc
Compression ratio 6.3:1
Carburettors 1/22 mm Mikuni
Maximum power 9.8 @ 6 000
Fuel tank 4.7 l

Transmission:
Gears/Clutch 5/wmp

Electrical:
Ignition 6 v/magneto
Starting kick

Notes: Also made as RV 50, RV 90, with 4-speed engines.

Braking:
Front/Rear 160 mm drums
Front tyres 5.4×14 road
Rear tyres 6.7×12 road

Suspension:
Front/Rear T/SA

Dimensions:
Ground clearance 165 mm
Seat height 730 mm
Wheelbase 1 305 mm
Overall length 1 960 mm
Dry weight 111 kg

Performance:
Top speed 96 km/h (p)
Fuel consumption ...

Suzuki FR70

Engine:
Type 2-str reed-valve single
Bore×Stroke 46×42 mm
Capacity 69 cc
Compression ratio 6.6:1
Carburettors 1/15 mm Mikuni
Maximum power 6.2 @ 6 500
Fuel tank 3.9 l

Transmission:
Gears/Clutch 3/A

Electrical:
Ignition 6 v/4 Ah/magneto
Starting kick

Notes:

Braking:
Front/Rear 130 mm drums
Front tyres 2.25×17 road
Rear tyres 2.25×17 road

Suspension:
Front/Rear LL/SA

Dimensions:
Ground clearance 140 mm
Seat height 762 mm
Wheelbase 1 180 mm
Overall length 1 825 mm
Dry weight 80 kg

Performance:
Top speed 78 km/h (p)
Fuel consumption 2.4 l/100 km (p)

Suzuki A50

Engine:
Type 2-str rotary-valve single
Bore×Stroke 41×37.8 mm
Capacity 49 cc
Compression ratio 7:1
Carburettors 1/16 mm Mikuni
Maximum power 4.8 @ 8 500
Fuel tank 6 l

Transmission:
Gears/Clutch 5/wmp

Electrical:
Ignition 6 v/4 Ah/magneto
Starting kick

Notes: AP50 is moped variant.

Braking:
Front/Rear 130 mm drums
Front tyres 2.25×17 road
Rear tyres 2.25×17 road

Suspension:
Front/Rear T/SA

Dimensions:
Ground clearance 150 mm
Seat height 830 mm
Wheelbase 1 185 mm
Overall length 1 800 mm
Dry weight 75 kg

Performance:
Top speed 70 km/h (p)
Fuel consumption ...

Suzuki started building motorcycles in 1952 with the introduction of its 36 cc 'Power Free' motorized bicycle, although previously it had been in textile engineering since its foundation by Michio Suzuki in 1909. In 1954 the company changed its name to Suzuki Motor Co. Ltd, and the pace of its growth then became phenomenal. Soon a wide range of 2-stroke motorcycles was joined by the manufacture of small cars, jeeps and vans, motorboats and outboard engines, bicycles and prefabricated housing units. There are now six production plants plus the wholly owned parts company at Akita, opened in 1973. Suzuki produces about 20 per cent of the $4\frac{1}{2}$ million bikes made in Japan each year and about half its production is exported around the world. Suzuki motorcycles are also assembled in Bangkok, Thailand.

The Suzuki range numbers some 40 models and includes many enduro and off-road versions which enjoy large sales in the North American market. Suzuki superbikes are used for police duties in several Australian cities and recently the company has offered the B120 as a lightweight police machine. Suzuki's debut in European racing came in 1960 and it quickly achieved world championship status in the 50 and 125 cc classes. Since 1970 it has raced full works teams with riders like Barry Sheene and Tepi Lansivuori on 500-fours and 750-triples, developing over 100 bhp and capable of speeds approaching 300 km/h. Suzuki was the first Japanese factory to compete in moto-cross and it has been by far the most successful, winning regularly in the 250 and 500 cc world championships.

Suzuki has always insisted on 2-stroke propulsion (although a 90 cc 4-stroke was made in 1954) and has pioneered many technical innovations such as the CCI lubrication system (see page 11), disc-valve induction (originally developed by MZ engineers), Ram-air cooling, designed to ensure that the engines of large 2-strokes run at the optimum temperature, and the adaptations of the rotary engine for motorcycle use. Typical of Japanese manufacturers, Suzuki has a large research and development section, and production models are constantly being adapted and modified in the light of the racing and competition experiences of the works teams. The company motto 'Make only valuable products' influences not only the constant search for new designs but also ensures the high standard of assembly work at the fully-automated factories of Toyama and Toyokawa.

Head Office: Suzuki Motor Co. Ltd, Hamamatsu-Nishi P.O. Box 1, Hamamatsu, 432–91 Japan.

UK Concessionaires: Suzuki GB Ltd, 87 Beddington Lane, Croydon, Surrey CR0 4TD.

Van Veen (The Netherlands)

OCR 1000

Engine:
Type 2-disc rotary
Bore × Stroke single chamber
Capacity 996 cc
Compression ratio 8.8:1
Carburettors 1/40 mm Weber
Maximum power 100 @ 6 500
Fuel tank 23 l

Transmission:
Gears/Clutch 4/2 dp

Electrical:
Ignition 12 v/ε/A
Starting electric

Notes: Shaft-driven and water cooled.

Braking:
Front/Rear 200 mm discs
Front tyres 3.50 × 18 road
Rear tyres 4.25 × 18 road

Suspension:
Front/Rear T/SA

Dimensions:
Ground clearance 100 mm
Seat height 795 mm
Wheelbase 1 495 mm
Overall length 2 170 mm
Dry weight 200 kg

Performance:
Top speed 240 km/h
Fuel consumption 10 l/100 km

Van Veen Import BV is the Dutch concessionaire for Kreidler mopeds and motorcycles and since 1965 has developed world championship-winning 50 cc, grand-prix racing bikes. The OCR-1000 project started in January 1972 as the personal hobby of H. Van Veen to produce an entirely new concept in superbikes. The engine chosen was the 'Comotor' a new rotary engine developed by Audi/NSU with the French Citroën company. This exciting power unit is said to be very flexible in use, capable of city-street pottering and high-speed motorway cruising, with exceptional acceleration where needed. Mechanically the engine is quiet and vibration-free and the high quality of the components used, which includes Bosch transistorized ignition and stainless-steel exhausts are expected to make this bike rather exclusive property. Factory production is expected to begin in 1976.

Head Office: Van Veen Import BV, Haarlemmerweg 518, Amsterdam 1015, The Netherlands.

Vélosolex (France) 3800

Engine:
Type 2-str single
Bore × Stroke 39.5 × 40 mm
Capacity 49 cc
Compression ratio 8.2:1
Carburettors 1/6.5 mm Solex
Maximum power 0.8 @ 3 800
Fuel tank 1.3 l

Transmission:
Gears/Clutch single/A

Electrical:
Ignition 6 v/magneto
Starting pedal

Notes:

Braking:
Front/Rear Caliper/89 mm dm
Front tyres 1.75 × 19 road
Rear tyres 1.75 × 19 road

Suspension:
Front/Rear T/rigid

Dimensions:
Ground clearance 150 mm
Seat height 790 mm
Wheelbase 990 mm
Overall length 1 610 mm
Dry weight 28 kg

Performance:
Top speed 40/km/h
Fuel consumption 1.3 l/100 km

Solex began making carburettors in 1910 and now claims to be the world's largest manufacturer. In 1946 Solex became part of S.I.N.F.A.C. (Société Industrielle Nouvelle de Fabrication pour l'Automobile et le Cycle) and shortly afterwards introduced the first autocycles. The Vélosolex factories are at Courbevoie, Arras and Tours and use highly automated assembly methods at every stage of manufacture. Output is 1 500 machines daily and some 5 million units have now been built since the first model was introduced. The Vélosolex is also manufactured under licence in three foreign countries.

The range includes the 4600 and 5000 models which feature quick engine lift by a crank-rod system and the Plisolex which folds completely in two with the engine disconnected. In France many students and housewives use this cheap and simple form of transport, and a nation-wide chain of Velosolex depots ensures an efficient sales and servicing organization for owners.

Head Office: S.I.N.F.A.C.–Vélosolex, 68, Boulevard de Verdon, 92 – Courbevoie, France.
UK Concessionaires: Harglo Ltd, 462 Station Road, Dorridge, Solihull.

Vespa (Italy)

Piaggio, manufacturer of Vespa scooters, Ciao and Brava mopeds, Gilera motorcycles and Vespa Commercial three-wheelers, is one of the world's largest producers of two-wheeled vehicles. The company was founded in 1884 as a ship's outfitters and subsequently diversified into the manufacture of railway carriages and aircraft. Between the wars Piaggio pioneered many technical advances in piston-engine aircraft construction and established a number of international air records. In 1943 the Pontedera bomber factory was destroyed by war action and in the chaos of reconstruction Piaggio conceived the idea of the motor scooter, a vehicle that was cheap and simple to run, yet combined the advantages of the car and of the motorcycle.

The Vespa was an immediate success and with Lambretta became a brand leader during the scooter boom of the sixties. Launched in 1946 the Vespa has since sold over 5 million units. From the scooter was derived the commercial three-wheeler which has sold widely in southern Italy and continues to play a major part in the transportation policies of less-developed countries. In 1967 Piaggio began the manufacture of mopeds and in 1969, following the resurgence in motorcycling, the company acquired the assets and name of Gilera (see page 71). The company also makes tractors and the KS 150 Hydrojet which is a jet-propelled motor for speedboats.

The Piaggio factories at Pontedera, Pisa and Arcore use the most modern methods of mass production, and output reaches about 450 000 units annually. About half this production is exported all over the world, with France, the Netherlands and West Germany being major sales outlets. Vespas are also produced under licence in Malaysia, Indonesia, Nigeria, Taiwan and Pakistan and there are assembly plants, using parts imported from Italy, in several African countries and Uruguay. In Europe, Moto Vespa SA of Spain have been making Piaggio products as a subsidiary for over twenty years and have an automated plant at Cuidad Lineal in Madrid (see page 175 for examples of Spanish-built Vespas and Gileras).

Piaggio products are well tried and excellently engineered and designed, and with the Vespa in the immediate post-war years and the three-wheelers in today's Third World the company can rightly claim to have made a significant social and economic contribution to the development of cheap and efficient transportation.

Head Office: Piaggio & Co. S.p.A., 16129 Genova – Via A. Cecchi, 6, Italy. Moto Vespa S.A., Julian Camarillo, 6, Madrid-17, Spain.

UK Concessionaires: Douglas Ltd., 2, Oak Lane, Fishponds, Bristol BS5 7XB.

Vespa by Piaggio

Engine:
Type 2-str rotary-valve single
Bore×Stroke 63.5×57 mm
Capacity 198 cc
Compression ratio 8.2:1
Carburettors 1/24 mm Dell'Orto
Maximum power 12.4 @ 5 700
Fuel tank 8 l

Transmission:
Gears/Clutch 4/wmp

Electrical:
Ignition 6 v/12 Ah/CD1/A
Starting kick

Notes: TL=trailing link front suspension.

Vespa by Piaggio

Engine:
Type 2-str rotary-valve single
Bore×Stroke 55×51 mm
Capacity 121.17 cc
Compression ratio 7.2:1
Carburettors 1/19 mm Dell'Orto
Maximum power 4.5 @ 5 700
Fuel tank 5.7 l

Transmission:
Gears/Clutch 4/direct drive

Electrical:
Ignition 6 v/magneto
Starting kick

Notes: Spare wheel fitted as standard.

Vespa by Piaggio

Engine:
Type 2-str rotary-valve single
Bore×Stroke 47×51 mm
Capacity 88.5 cc
Compression ratio 7.2:1
Carburettors 1/16 mm Dell'Orto
Maximum power 3.1 @ 5 200
Fuel tank 5 l

Transmission:
Gears/Clutch 3/direct drive

Electrical:
Ignition 6 v/magneto
Starting kick

Notes: Scooter range also includes 150 super.

Electronic 200

Braking:
Front/Rear 152 mm drums
Front tyres 3.50×10 road
Rear tyres 3.50×10 road

Suspension:
Front/Rear TL/SA

Dimensions:
Ground clearance 225 mm
Seat height 787 mm
Wheelbase 1 232 mm
Overall length [a] 1 778 mm
Dry weight 104 kg

Performance:
Top speed 110 km/h
Fuel consumption 3 l/100 km

125 Primavera

Braking:
Front/Rear 120 mm dm/146 mm dm
Front tyres 3.00×10 road
Rear tyres 3.00×10 road

Suspension:
Front/Rear Springs/shock absorbers

Dimensions:
Ground clearance 225 mm
Seat height 787 mm
Wheelbase 1 180 mm
Overall length 1 665 mm
Dry weight 73 kg

Performance:
Top speed 85 km/h
Fuel consumption 2 l/100 km

90 Standard

Braking:
Front/Rear 127 mm dm/133 mm dm
Front tyres 3.10×10 road
Rear tyres 3.10×10 road

Suspension:
Front/Rear Springs/shock absorbers

Dimensions:
Ground clearance 225 mm
Seat height 787 mm
Wheelbase 1 180 mm
Overall length 1 665 mm
Dry weight 73 kg

Performance:
Top speed 70 km/h
Fuel consumption 1.9 l/100 km

Vespa by Piaggio

Engine:
Type   2-str rotary-valve single
Bore × Stroke   38.4 × 43 mm
Capacity   49 cc
Compression ratio   7.2:1
Carburettors   1/12 mm Dell'Orto
Maximum power   1.4 @ 5 000
Fuel tank   5 l

Transmission:
Gears/Clutch   3/direct drive

Electrical:
Ignition   6 v/magneto
Starting   pedal

Notes:

Vespa by Piaggio

Engine:
Type   2-str horizontal single
Bore × stroke   38.4 × 43 mm
Capacity   49.77 cc
Compression ratio   8:1
Carburettors   1/12 mm Dell'Orto
Maximum power   1.25 @ 4 500
Fuel tank   6.5 l

Transmission:
Gears/Clutch   variable/A

Electrical:
Ignition   6 v/magneto
Starting   pedal

Notes:

Vespa by Piaggio

Engine:
Type   2-str rotary-valve single
Bore × Stroke   38.4 × 43 mm
Capacity   49.77 cc
Compression ratio   8:1
Carburettors   1/12 mm Dell'Orto
Maximum power   1.25 @ 4 500
Fuel tank   2.8 l

Transmission:
Gears/Clutch   single/A

Electrical:
Ignition   6 v/magneto
Starting   pedal

Notes: V model has variable speed. Brava and Boxer are other moped models.

50 moped

Braking:
Front/Rear   127 mm dm/133 mm dm
Front tyres   2.75 × 9 road
Rear tyres   2.75 × 9 road

Suspension:
Front/Rear   Springs/shock absorbers

Dimensions:
Ground clearance   210 mm
Seat height   787 mm
Wheelbase   1 155 mm
Overall length   1 630 mm
Dry weight   66 kg

Performance:
Top speed   48 km/h
Fuel consumption   1.3 l/100 km

Vespino Tourist Rally

Braking:
Front/Rear   89 mm dm/133 mm dm
Front tyres   2.25 × 18 road
Rear tyres   2.25 × 18 road

Suspension:
Front/Rear   T/SA

Dimensions:
Ground clearance   ...
Seat height   ...
Wheelbase   ...
Overall length   ...
Dry weight   52 kg

Performance:
Top speed   40 km/h
Fuel consumption   1.5 l/100 km

Ciao V/E

Braking:
Front/Rear   89 mm dm/133 mm dm
Front tyres   2.00 × 17 road
Rear tyres   2.00 × 17 road

Suspension:
Front/Rear   LL/rigid

Dimensions:
Ground clearance   180 mm
Seat height   770 mm
Wheelbase   1 000 mm
Overall length   1 640 mm
Dry weight   39 kg

Performance:
Top speed   40 km/h
Fuel consumption   1.3 l/100 km

Moto Vespa

GT 160

Engine:
Type 2-str rotary-valve single
Bore × Stroke 60 × 57 mm
Capacity 161.16 cc
Compression ratio 8 : 1
Carburettors 1/19 mm Arbeo
Maximum power 7.8 @ 5 200
Fuel tank 7.7 l

Transmission:
Gears/Clutch 4/direct drive

Electrical:
Ignition 12 v/ε/A
Starting kick

Notes:

Braking:
Front/Rear 150 mm drums
Front tyres 3.50 × 10 road
Rear tyres 3.50 × 10 road

Suspension:
Front/Rear Springs/shock absorbers

Dimensions:
Ground clearance 240 mm
Seat height ...
Wheelbase 1 240 mm
Overall length 1 780 mm
Dry weight 98 kg

Performance:
Top speed 90 km/h
Fuel consumption 2.5 l/100 km

Moto Vespa

Vespino GL

Engine:
Type 2-str horizontal single
Bore × Stroke 38.4 × 43 mm
Capacity 49.77 cc
Compression ratio 8 : 1
Carburettors 1/12 mm Arbeo
Maximum power 2.2 @ 4 700
Fuel tank 3.3 l

Transmission:
Gears/Clutch variable/A

Electrical:
Ignition 6 v/magneto
Starting pedal

Notes:

Braking:
Front/Rear 90 mm dm/150 mm dm
Front tyres 2.25 × 18 road
Rear tyres 2.25 × 18 road

Suspension:
Front/Rear T/SA

Dimensions:
Ground clearance ...
Seat height ...
Wheelbase 1 330 mm
Overall length 1 760 mm
Dry weight 52 kg

Performance:
Top speed 40 km/h
Fuel consumption 1.6 l/100 km

Moto Vespa

Gilera

Engine:
Type 2-str single
Bore × Stroke 38.4 × 43 mm
Capacity 49.75 cc
Compression ratio 6.5 : 1
Carburettors 1/14 mm Arbeo
Maximum power 2 @ 5 000
Fuel tank 3.2 l

Transmission:
Gears/Clutch 4/wmp

Electrical:
Ignition 6 v/magneto
Starting pedal

Notes:

Braking:
Front/Rear 102 mm drums
Front tyres 2.50 × 17 road
Rear tyres 2.50 × 17 road

Suspension:
Front/Rear T/SA

Dimensions:
Ground clearance 180 mm
Seat height 800 mm
Wheelbase 1 095 mm
Overall length 1 690 mm
Dry weight 52 kg

Performance:
Top speed 40 km/h
Fuel consumption 1.6 l/100 km

Yamaha (Japan) — XS 650B

Engine:
Type 4-str ohc twin
Bore×Stroke 75×74 mm
Capacity 653 cc
Compression ratio 8.4:1
Carburettors 2/38 mm Mikuni
Maximum power 53 @ 7 500
Fuel tank 15 l

Transmission:
Gears/Clutch 5/wmp

Electrical:
Ignition 12 v/14 Ah/b&c/A
Starting electric

Notes:

Braking:
Front/Rear 260 mm dc/180 mm dm
Front tyres 3.50×19 road
Rear tyres 4.00×18 road

Suspension:
Front/Rear T/SA (5-pos.)

Dimensions:
Ground clearance 140 mm
Seat height 800 mm
Wheelbase 1 435 mm
Overall length 2 180 mm
Dry weight 214 kg

Performance:
Top speed 185 km/h
Fuel consumption …

Yamaha — XS 500B

Engine:
Type 4-str dohc twin
Bore×Stroke 73×59.6 mm
Capacity 498 cc
Compression ratio 8.5:1
Carburettors 2/32 mm Mikuni
Maximum power 48 @ 8 500
Fuel tank 16 l

Transmission:
Gears/Clutch 5/wmp

Electrical:
Ignition 12 v/14 Ah/b&c/A
Starting electric

Notes:

Braking:
Front/Rear 267 mm dc/190 mm dm
Front tyres 3.25×19 road
Rear tyres 3.50×18 road

Suspension:
Front/Rear T/SA (5-pos.)

Dimensions:
Ground clearance 155 mm
Seat height 800 mm
Wheelbase 1 410 mm
Overall length 2 150 mm
Dry weight 190 kg

Performance:
Top speed 180 km/h
Fuel consumption …

Yamaha — RD 350B

Engine:
Type 2-str reed-valve twin
Bore×Stroke 64×54 mm
Capacity 347 cc
Compression ratio 6.6:1
Carburettors 2/28 mm Mikuni
Maximum power 39 @ 7 500
Fuel tank 15 l

Transmission:
Gears/Clutch 6/wmp

Electrical:
Ignition 12 v/5 Ah/b&c/A
Starting kick

Notes:

Braking:
Front/Rear 267 mm dc/178 mm dm
Front tyres 3.00×18 road
Rear tyres 3.50×18 road

Suspension:
Front/Rear T/SA (3-pos.)

Dimensions:
Ground clearance 190 mm
Seat height 787 mm
Wheelbase 1 346 mm
Overall length 2 057 mm
Dry weight 151 kg

Performance:
Top speed 160 km/h
Fuel consumption 7 l/100 km (p)

Yamaha RD 250

Engine:
Type 2-str reed-valve twin†
Bore × Stroke 54 × 54 mm
Capacity 247 cc
Compression ratio 6.7 : 1
Carburettors 2/28 mm Mikuni
Maximum power 30 @ 7 500
Fuel tank 16 l

Transmission:
Gears/Clutch 5/wmp

Electrical:
Ignition 12 v/b&c/A
Starting kick

Notes: †Torque induction

Braking:
Front/Rear 267 mm dc/180 mm dm
Front tyres 3.00 × 18 road
Rear tyres 3.50 × 18 road

Suspension:
Front/Rear T/SA

Dimensions:
Ground clearance 150 mm
Seat height 800 mm
Wheelbase 1 320 mm
Overall length 2 040 mm
Dry weight 140 kg

Performance:
Top speed 160 km/h
Fuel consumption 2.5 l/100 km

Yamaha RD 200B

Engine:
Type 2-str twin†
Bore × Stroke 52 × 46 mm
Capacity 195 cc
Compression ratio 7.1 : 1
Carburettors 2/20 mm Mikuni
Maximum power 22 @ 7 500
Fuel tank 11.5 l

Transmission:
Gears/Clutch 5/wmp

Electrical:
Ignition 12 v/b&c/D
Starting electric

Notes: †Torque Induction. Also RD50DX, RD125B and RD250B models.

Braking:
Front/Rear 180 mm dm/150 mm dm
Front tyres 2.75 × 18 road
Rear tyres 3.00 × 18 road

Suspension:
Front/Rear T/SA

Dimensions:
Ground clearance 155 mm
Seat height 770 mm
Wheelbase 1 245 mm
Overall length 1 945 mm
Dry weight 116 kg

Performance:
Top speed 133 km/h
Fuel consumption 2.8 l/100 km

Yamaha RS 125B

Engine:
Type 2-str single†
Bore × Stroke 56 × 50 mm
Capacity 123 cc
Compression ratio 6.9 : 1
Carburettors 1/24 mm Mikuni
Maximum power 12.5 @ 8 000
Fuel tank 9 l

Transmission:
Gears/Clutch 5/wmp

Electrical:
Ignition 6 v/magneto
Starting kick

Notes: †Torque Induction. Also RS 100B model.

Braking:
Front/Rear 150 mm dm/130 mm dm
Front tyres 2.75 × 18 road
Rear tyres 2.75 × 18 road

Suspension:
Front/Rear T/SA

Dimensions:
Ground clearance 150 mm
Seat height 770 mm
Wheelbase 1 205 mm
Overall length 1 870 mm
Dry weight 93 kg

Performance:
Top speed 118 km/h
Fuel consumption 2.2 l/100 km

Yamaha — YB100B

Engine:
Type 2-str rotary-valve single
Bore×Stroke 52×45.6 mm
Capacity 96 cc
Compression ratio 7.2:1
Carburettors 1/22 mm Mikuni
Maximum power 9.5 @ 7 500
Fuel tank 9.3 l

Transmission:
Gears/Clutch 4/wmp

Electrical:
Ignition 6 v/magneto
Starting kick

Notes: Also YB50B, YB80B and YB125B models.

Braking:
Front/Rear 110 mm drums
Front tyres 2.50×18 road
Rear tyres 2.75×18 road

Suspension:
Front/Rear T/SA

Dimensions:
Ground clearance 140 mm
Seat height 730 mm
Wheelbase 1 190 mm
Overall length 1 915 mm
Dry weight 92 kg

Performance:
Top speed 110 km/h
Fuel consumption 2 l/100 km

Yamaha — YGIFD80

Engine:
Type 2-str rotary-valve single
Bore×Stroke 47×42 mm
Capacity 73 cc
Compression ratio 6.8:1
Carburettors 1/18 mm Mikuni
Maximum power 7 @ 7 000
Fuel tank 6.5 l

Transmission:
Gears/Clutch 4/wmp

Electrical:
Ignition 6 v/magneto
Starting kick

Notes:

Braking:
Front/Rear 110 mm drums
Front tyres 2.50×17 road
Rear tyres 2.50×17 road

Suspension:
Front/Rear T/SA

Dimensions:
Ground clearance 150 mm
Seat height 770 mm
Wheelbase 1 145 mm
Overall length 1 815 mm
Dry weight 72 kg

Performance:
Top speed 86 km/h
Fuel consumption ...

Yamaha — FSIE

Engine:
Type 2-str rotary-valve single
Bore×Stroke 40×39.7 mm
Capacity 49 cc
Compression ratio 7.1:1
Carburettors 1/16 mm Mikuni
Maximum power 4.8 @ 7 000
Fuel tank 6 l

Transmission:
Gears/Clutch 4/wmp

Electrical:
Ignition 6 v/magneto
Starting pedal

Notes:

Braking:
Front/Rear 110 mm drums
Front tyres 2.25×17 road
Rear tyres 2.50×17 road

Suspension:
Front/Rear T/SA

Dimensions:
Ground clearance 135 mm
Seat height 770 mm
Wheelbase 1 160 mm
Overall length 1 755 mm
Dry weight 70 kg

Performance:
Top speed 73 km/h
Fuel consumption 1.5 l/100 km

Yamaha — V70A

Engine:
Type 2-str reed-valve single
Bore×Stroke 47×42 mm
Capacity 72 cc
Compression ratio 6.8:1
Carburettors ...
Maximum power 6.2 @ 6 500
Fuel tank 5.3 l

Transmission:
Gears/Clutch 2/A

Electrical:
Ignition 6 v/magneto
Starting kick

Notes: Also as V50 and V90.

Braking:
Front/Rear 110 mm drums
Front tyres 2.25×17 road
Rear tyres 2.25×17 road

Suspension:
Front/Rear LL/SA

Dimensions:
Ground clearance 130 mm
Seat height 760 mm
Wheelbase 1 170 mm
Overall length 1 840 mm
Dry weight 75 kg

Performance:
Top speed 85 km/h
Fuel consumption ...

Yamaha — GT 50B

Engine:
Type 2-str reed-valve single
Bore×Stroke 40×39.7 mm
Capacity 49 cc
Compression ratio 6.8:1
Carburettors 1/16 mm Mikuni
Maximum power 4 @ 7 500
Fuel tank 4.8 l

Transmission:
Gears/Clutch 4/wmp

Electrical:
Ignition 6 v/magneto
Starting kick

Notes: Also GT 80B model.

Braking:
Front/Rear 110 mm drums
Front tyres 2.50×15 trials
Rear tyres 2.75×14 trials

Suspension:
Front/Rear T/SA

Dimensions:
Ground clearance 195 mm
Seat height 655 mm
Wheelbase 1 045 mm
Overall length 1 635 mm
Dry weight 63 kg

Performance:
Top speed 70 km/h
Fuel consumption 1.5 l/100 km

Yamaha — DT 400B

Engine:
Type 2-str singlet†
Bore×Stroke 85×70 mm
Capacity 397 cc
Compression ratio 6.4:1
Carburettors 1/32 mm Mikuni
Maximum power 20 @ 5 500
Fuel tank 9 l

Transmission:
Gears/Clutch 5/wmp

Electrical:
Ignition 6 v/CDI/magneto
Starting kick

Notes: †Torque Induction. Also DT 100B, 125B, 125EB, 175B and 250B models.

Braking:
Front/Rear 160 mm dm/150 mm dm
Front tyres 3.00×21 trials
Rear tyres 4.00×18 trials

Suspension:
Front/Rear T/SA

Dimensions:
Ground clearance 220 mm
Seat height 815 mm
Wheelbase 1 425 mm
Overall length 2 180 mm
Dry weight 125 kg

Performance:
Top speed 130 km/h
Fuel consumption 2.8 l/100 km

The short but brilliant career of the Yamaha Motor Co. can be traced through a succession of models, each incorporating performance improvements and technical innovations derived from the company's elaborate research and development programme and proved through its aggressive racing commitment. In 1955 Yamaha, having made organs and pianos since 1887, produced its first motorcycle, the 125 cc YA1. A new factory was soon commissioned and 175 and 5-speed 250 cc models with double-cradle frames were included in the Yamaha range, along with a moped and a 173 cc 2-speed scooter. The 1961 YA5 was the first use of a rotary-valve engine in production machines, and the Autolube oiling injection system and reed valves were introduced on 1964 models. The 125 cc YAS1 of 1967 featured a 5-port engine to improve operating efficiency, and torque induction with a 7th port assembly was fitted to the 1971 trail models. With the introduction of the big 4-stroke twins in 1972 Yamaha produced the Omni-Phase Balancer to help suppress crankshaft vibrations, and the following year saw the first appearance of the dohc 8-valve engine. A recent revolutionary design is the Monocross suspension developed for Yamaha's moto-cross range.

This constant model improvement and careful attention to styling have given Yamaha the reputation of being the trendsetter amongst the world's motorcycle manufacturers. Much of the high technology of Yamaha bikes is first proved in competition by the works racing teams. Yamaha began serious racing in 1961 and by 1964 was regularly winning world championships in the 125 and 250 cc classes. The latest TZ 750B road racers develop over 90 bhp and are capable of speeds in excess of 265 km/h and have dominated the Daytona 200 in recent years.

Yamaha bikes are made at Iwata, south-west of Tokyo, and production exceeds a million units annually, representing some 25 per cent of Japan's total motorcycle production. Over half the Yamaha output is exported and there is a number of overseas assembly plants. An important market for the 30-odd Yamaha models is the USA. In addition to motorcycles Yamaha also makes snowmobiles, outboard motors, fibre-glass power boats and yachts and swimming pools. A recent activity has been the development and administration of various leisure complexes such as the Sugo Motor Centre which contains a moto-cross course, a trail course, a kart track and a road-racing circuit all on one site. Yamaha also operates the only training school in Japan specifically designed for motorcycles. The parent company Nippon Gakki, is the world's largest manufacturer of musical instruments.

Head Office: Yamaha Motor Co. Ltd, 2500 Shingai, Iwata-shi, Shizuoka-ken, Japan.

UK Concessionaires: Mitzui Machinery Sales (UK) Ltd, Oakcroft Road, Chessington, Surrey KT9 1SA.

Yankee (USA)

500Z

Engine:
Type 2-str vertical twin
Bore × Stroke 72 × 60 mm
Capacity 488 cc
Compression ratio 11.5 : 1
Carburettors 2/27 mm IRZ
Maximum power 36 @ 6 500
Fuel tank 9.5 l

Transmission:
Gears/Clutch 6/dmp

Electrical:
Ignition 6 v/6 Ah/:/A
Starting kick

Notes:

Braking:
Front/Rear 150 mm dm/225 mm dc
Front tyres 3.15 × 21 trials
Rear tyres 4.20 × 18 trials

Suspension:
Front/Rear T/SA (5-pos.)

Dimensions:
Ground clearance 208 mm
Seat height 775 mm
Wheelbase 1 397 mm
Overall length 2 159 mm
Dry weight 146 kg

Performance:
Top speed 144 km/h
Fuel consumption 8 l/100 km

The Yankee 500 twin, the first new, American-built motorcycle to appear since the last war, was introduced in 1972. Mechanically the bike is based on two 250 cc Ossa Pioneer singles, sharing a common crankcase, but it is built to very precise specifications and is assembled with high-quality components. The Yankee 500Z is an ISDT type machine and an unusual design feature is the front drum and rear disc-brake arrangement. The bikes are built in Schenectady, New York, and the design was inspired by John Taylor, an Ossa distributor in the USA. A 500SS street-scrambler version fitted with road tyres, front disc brakes and an oil-injection system is being prepared by the Ossa factory in Barcelona, Spain.
Head Office: Yankee Motor Company, P.O. Box, 36, Schenectady, New York 12301, USA.

Zündapp (West Germany) — KS 125 Sport

Engine:
Type 2-str single
Bore × Stroke 54 × 54 mm
Capacity 123 cc
Compression ratio 12.4 : 1
Carburettors 1/27 mm Bing
Maximum power 17 @ 7 600
Fuel tank 14.25 l

Transmission:
Gears/Clutch 5/wmp

Electrical:
Ignition 6 v/12 Ah/ε/D
Starting kick

Notes: GS moto-cross model also available (see p. 189).

Braking:
Front/Rear 150 mm drums
Front tyres 2.75 × 18 road
Rear tyres 3.25 × 18 road

Suspension:
Front/Rear T/SA (3-pos.)

Dimensions:
Ground clearance 130 mm
Seat height 770 mm
Wheelbase 1 325 mm
Overall length 2 010 mm
Dry weight 116 kg

Performance:
Top speed 120 km/h
Fuel consumption 5 l/100 km

Zündapp — KS 50 Water-Cooled

Engine:
Type 2-str single
Bore × Stroke 39 × 41.8 mm
Capacity 49.9 cc
Compression ratio 9 : 1
Carburettors 1/19 mm Bing
Maximum power 6.25 @ 8 400
Fuel tank 11.25 l

Transmission:
Gears/Clutch 5/wmp

Electrical:
Ignition 6 v/6 Ah/ε/D
Starting kick

Notes: Also available as Super Sport and Cross model.

Braking:
Front/Rear 150 mm drums
Front tyres 2.75 × 17 road
Rear tyres 2.75 × 17 road

Suspension:
Front/Rear T/SA

Dimensions:
Ground clearance 130 mm
Seat height 770 mm
Wheelbase 1 250 mm
Overall length 1 900 mm
Dry weight 88 kg

Performance:
Top speed 85 km/h
Fuel consumption 2.85 l/100 km

Zündapp — RS 50

Engine:
Type 2-str single
Bore × Stroke 39 × 41.8 mm
Capacity 49.9 cc
Compression ratio 9 : 1
Carburettors 1/16 mm Bing
Maximum power 2.9 @ 4 900
Fuel tank 7.5 l

Transmission:
Gears/Clutch 3/wmp

Electrical:
Ignition 6 v/magneto
Starting kick

Notes: 4-speed super model develops 4.6 bhp

Braking:
Front/Rear 120 mm drums
Front tyres 3.00 × 10 road
Rear tyres 3.00 × 10 road

Suspension:
Front/Rear LL/SA

Dimensions:
Ground clearance
Seat height 760 mm
Wheelbase 1 230 mm
Overall length 1 775 mm
Dry weight 83 kg

Performance:
Top speed 40 km/h
Fuel consumption 2.3 l/100 km

Zündapp M50

Engine:
Type 2-str fan single
Bore × Stroke 39 × 41.8 mm
Capacity 49.9 cc
Compression ratio 8.1:1
Carburettors 1/16 mm Bing
Maximum power 2.5 @ 4 800
Fuel tank 5 l

Transmission:
Gears/Clutch 2/wmp

Electrical:
Ignition 6 v/magneto
Starting pedal

Notes: Also M25 with detuned engine.

Braking:
Front/Rear 90 mm drums
Front tyres 2.25 × 23 road
Rear tyres 2.25 × 23 road

Suspension:
Front/Rear LL/SA

Dimensions:
Ground clearance ...
Seat height 777 mm
Wheelbase 1 168 mm
Overall length 1 860 mm
Dry weight 50 kg

Performance:
Top speed 40 km/h
Fuel consumption 1.65 l/100 km

The Zünder-und-Apparatebau company was founded by Fritz Neumeyer in 1917 at Nürnberg to make fuses for artillery guns. After World War I the company began making motorcycles and its first model, a 211 cc 2-stroke, appeared in 1921. In the thirties Zündapp produced a range from 175 to 800 cc, light delivery vehicles, aero engines and a Porsche-designed 'people's car'. A technical breakthrough of the time was a three-way scavenging system later to be widely used in high-performance 2-strokes. After World War II, Zündapp was temporarily a sewing machine manufacturer but from 1947 produced 600 cc shaft-driven flat-twins. In the fifties the Bella scooters appeared and production was moved to Munich. From the start Zündapp has been very interested in cross-country and endurance trials and its machines hold many world records. Today Zündapp is Germany's largest motorcycle manufacturer and the range includes mopeds, lightweight roadsters and moto-cross machines up to 360 cc, and a newly introduced electric-powered moped.

Head Office: Zündapp-Werke GmbH, 8 München 80, Anzinger Str 1–3, West Germany.
UK Concessionaires: Zündapp UK, 34a High Road Beeston, Sandy, Bedfordshire.

Zündapp Automatic

Engine:
Type: 2-str single
Bore × Stroke 39 × 41.8 mm
Capacity 49.9 cc
Compression ratio 10.5:1
Carburettors 1/10 mm Bing
Maximum power 1.5 @ 4 200
Fuel tank 3 l

Transmission:
Gears/Clutch single/A

Electrical:
Ignition 6 v/magneto
Starting pedal

Notes: Variety of moped models available.

Braking:
Front/Rear 80 mm drums
Front tyres 2.00 × 17 road
Rear tyres 2.00 × 17 road

Suspension:
Front/Rear T/rigid

Dimensions:
Ground clearance ...
Seat height 780–870 mm
Wheelbase 1 105 mm
Overall length 1 705 mm
Dry weight 39 kg

Performance:
Top speed 25 km/h
Fuel consumption 1.5 l/100 km

Zundapp GS 125 cc Enduro

Models Compared

The 125s

	Benelli 125 2C	Harley SS 125	Honda CB 125 J	Kawasaki 125B	Maico MD125
Engine	2-str	2-str	4-str	2-str	2-str
Cylinders	2	1	1	1	1
Capacity (cc)	125	123	122	124	125
Comp. ratio	10.1	10.8	9.5	6.4	11.1
Power (bhp)	15	...	14	13	16
Tank (l)	13	8.5	7.5	8.5	13.5
Voltage	6	12	6	12	6
Starting	K	K	K	K	K
Gears	5	5	5	4	6
Clutch	wmp	wmp	wmp	wmp	wmp
Front Brakes	dm	dm	dc	dm	dm
Rear Brakes	dm	dm	dm	dm	dm
Front Tyres	2.75×18	3.00×19	2.75×18	3.00×16	2.50×16
Rear Tyres	3.00×18	3.50×18	3.00×18	3.00×16	3.00×16
Weight (kg)	115	109	91	117	99
Speed (km/h)	112	105	112	112	123
l/100 km	4	...	3	...	5

	Motoconfort 125 LT	MV Agusta 125 Sport	Suzuki TS 125	Yamaha RS 125B	Zündapp KS 125
Engine	2-str	4-str	2-str	2-str	2-str
Cylinders	2	1	1	1	1
Capacity (cc)	125	123	123	123	123
Comp. ratio	11.1	9.5	6.7	7.0	12.4
Power (bhp)	16	14	14	12.5	17
Tank (l)	13	14	7	9	14
Voltage	6	12	6	6	6
Starting	K	K	K	K	K
Gears	5	5	5	5	5
Clutch	wmp	wmp	wmp	wmp	wmp
Front Brakes	dm	dc	dm	dm	dm
Rear Brakes	dm	dm	dm	dm	dm
Front Tyres	2.50×17	2.75×18	2.75×21	2.75×18	2.75×18
Rear Tyres	3.00×17	4.00×18	3.25×18	2.75×18	3.25×18
Weight (kg)	...	103	90	93	116
Speed (km/h)	...	120	105	118	120
l/100 km	...	3.1	4.6	2.2	5

The 250s

	Benelli 250 2C	Bultaco Metralla	CZ 250 Sport	Harley D SS 250	Honda CB 250
Engine	4-str	2-str	2-str	2-str	4-str
Cylinders	2	1	2	1	2
Capacity (cc)	231	244	246	243	249
Comp. ratio	10.0	10.0	9.3	10.3	9.5
Power (bhp)	25	23	17	...	27
Tank (l)	13	13	13	11	11
Voltage	6	6	6	12	12
Starting	K	K	K	K	E
Gears	5	5	4	5	6
Clutch	wmp	wmp	wmp	wmp	wmp
Front Brakes	dm	dm	dm	dm	dc
Rear Brakes	dm	dm	dm	dm	dm
Front Tyres	3.00×18	3.25×19	3.00×18	3.25×19	3.00×18
Rear Tyres	3.25×18	3.50×18	3.25×18	4.00×18	3.50×18
Weight (kg)	144	118	142	136	165
Speed (km/h)	148	145	120	136	132
l/100 km	5.0	...	4.2	4.2	4.6

	Kawasaki 250 KH	Moto-Guzzi 250 TS	MZ TS 250	Suzuki GT 250A	Yamaha RD 250
Engine	2-str	2-str	2-str	2-str	2-str
Cylinders	3	2	1	2	2
Capacity (cc)	249	231	249	247	247
Comp. ratio	7.5	10.0	9.5	7.5	6.7
Power (bhp)	28	30	21	33	30
Tank (l)	14	13	19	15	16
Voltage	12	6	6	12	12
Starting	K	K	K	K	K
Gears	5	5	4	6	5
Clutch	wmp	wmp	wmp	wmp	wmp
Front Brakes	dc	dm	dm	dc	dc
Rear Brakes	dm	dm	dm	dm	dm
Front Tyres	3.25×18	3.00×18	3.00×16	3.00×18	3.00×18
Rear Tyres	3.50×18	3.25×18	3.50×16	3.25×18	3.50×18
Weight (kg)	155	129	118	146	140
Speed (km/h)	144	142	128	152	160
l/100 km	6.4	7.0	5.0	5.6	7.0

The 500s

	Honda CB 500T	Kawasaki H150	Ducati 500 GTL	Suzuki GT 500A	Yamaha XS 500B
Engine	4-str	2-str	4-str	2-str	4-str
Cylinders	2	3	2	2	2
Capacity (cc)	498	498	497	492	498
Comp. ratio	8.5	6.8	10.0	6.6	8.5
Power (bhp)	42	59	39.5	44	48
Tank (l)	16	16	19	16	16
Voltage	12	12	12	12	12
Starting	E	K	E	K	E
Gears	5	5	5	5	5
Clutch	wmp	wmp	wmp	wmp	wmp
Front Brakes	dc	dc	dc	dc	dc
Rear Brakes	dm	dm	dm	dm	dm
Front Tyres	3.25×19	3.25×19	3.25×18	3.25×19	3.25×19
Rear Tyres	3.75×18	4.00×18	3.50×18	4.00×18	4.00×18
Weight (kg)	193	185	172	187	190
Speed (km/h)	163	180	172	176	180
l/100 km	5.5	8.0	3.85	6.3	...

The 750s

	Benelli 750 Sei	Honda 750 Four	MV Agusta 750S	NVT T160	Suzuki GT 750A
Engine	4-str	4-str	4-str	4-str	2-str
Cylinders	6	4	4	2	3
Capacity (cc)	747	736	743	748	740
Comp. ratio	9.0	9.0	10.0	9.5	6.7
Power (bhp)	76	67	80	72	70
Tank (l)	23	17	24	19	17
Voltage	12	12	12	12	12
Starting	E	E	K	E	E
Gears	5	5	5	5	5
Clutch	wmp	wmp	wmp	wmp	wmp
Front Brakes	dc	dc	dc	dc	dc
Rear Brakes	dm	dm	dm	dc	dc
Front Tyres	3.50×18	3.25×19	3.50×18	3.50×19	3.25×19
Rear Tyres	4.50×18	4.00×18	4.00×18	3.50×19	4.00×18
Weight (kg)	236	218	230	191	230
Speed (km/h)	195	185	225	220	200
l/100 km	8.0	6.0	8.0	5.5	6.4